Autism, Amalgam and Me
Jodi's Journey Continues

(the link between autism and mercury)

By

Jean Shaw

Disclaimer and Terms of Use:

The Author and Publisher has strived to be as accurate and complete as possible in the creation of this book, notwithstanding the fact she does not warrant or represent at any time the contents within are accurate due to the rapidly changing nature of the Internet, and the advances in health, science and technology.

While all attempts have been made to verify information provided in this publication, the Author and Publisher assumes no responsibility for errors, omissions, or contrary interpretation of the subject matter herein.

Any perceived slights of specific persons, peoples, or organizations are unintentional. Readers are advised to seek the services of competent professionals in all health matters and the information within this book is for educational purposes only.

Liability Disclaimer

By reading this book, you assume all risks associated with using the advice given below, with a full understanding that you, solely, are responsible for anything that may occur as a result of putting this information into action in any way, and regardless of your interpretation of the advice.

Copyright

Printed in the United States of America

Dedication

With thanks to Pam and Bryan for pointing us in the right direction and special thanks to Jodi's grandparents for always being there.

Reflections

Sitting at the keyboard,
Reflecting on my life,
I'm sure I could be so much more
Than just a mother and a wife.

I think in the great scheme of things
As part of the Master Plan,
Each one has a role to play
To help his fellow man.

I don't know what my task is,
What I'm supposed to do,
But now I'm half way through my life,
I hope to find a clue.

I know it won't be very much,
My star sign isn't right.
I'm Pisces, indecisive,
No opinions and no fight.

I'm very easy going,
Don't get angry, never fuss,
Won't argue, don't hold grudges
Hardly awe inspiring stuff.

But someday, somehow, somewhere,
I'll do something with my life,
So I won't just die as Jean Shaw
The mother and the wife!

Autism, Amalgam and Me
Jodi's Journey Continues

By

Jean Shaw

Table of Contents

Foreword

Firstly let me make something absolutely clear. I am not a scientist, have no medical training and did not study for any degrees. The knowledge I am about to impart comes from the School of Life – my life!

It has been gained through necessity rather than desire, and the information in this book is for educational purposes only.

It is neither meant to diagnose, treat or cure any known illness and if you have any specific health concerns you must ALWAYS consult your health practitioner.

That said I hope this book will save you hours of research and point you in the direction of help should you need it.

There is a lot of information and misinformation out there.

PLEASE check things out for yourself and make your own mind up.

Introduction

If you haven't read my first book called, I'm Not Naughty – I'm Autistic – Jodi's Journey, I'd better introduce myself.

I am Jodi's mum and this book, unlike the original, has been written as though narrated by both Jodi and myself.

My son Jodi has autism and does not use language. He uses odd words, which is not quite the same thing, but manages to convey a great deal of information nevertheless.

This book deals with two different subjects; why I think Jodi is autistic and mercury toxicity caused by dental amalgam.

It continues from where the last story ended, and has been written partly because of genuine interest in Jodi, but mostly because of an amazing sequence of events, which have proved incredibly beneficial to our lives.

We will share them with you so you can see how the two topics are connected.

If you're interested, read on …

Jodi - 1

Well, here I am – back by popular demand. That's probably putting it a bit strong but several people have been genuinely interested in me and have asked my secretary, (good old mum), when the next book is coming out.

Anyway, the fact you're reading this most likely means you want to know how I'm getting on now I'm a fully fledged teenager. Well, at the ripe old age of fourteen years I'm much different from when I was a mere child of twelve.

My voice has broken for a start and when it first started to change my mum kept asking if I had a sore throat. Of course, I didn't answer her so she kept putting her hand on my head to see if I had a temperature and checking in my mouth for signs of a white tongue or red tonsils.

It's a major problem when mum suspects I'm ill because I can't tell her how I feel or what hurts. She just goes through the motions of checking for any visible signs of illness or pain, and if I'm off my food and drink, have a change of temperament, or sleep more than usual, she takes me to the doctor for an expert opinion.

With the voice episode though it was just the sounds coming from my mouth which regularly changed tone and sounded really strange, and bearing in mind my brother, who is only twenty one months older than me, had relatively recently been through the voice breaking stage, it was a bit surprising my Mum was so slow in picking up the signs.

However, it's not that surprising because many people wrongly assume a person with a disability won't develop as quickly as so called "normal" people do, whereas many actually develop earlier. Also along those lines it's amazing how many people talk down to disabled people – well, me anyway, as if I'm a baby.

I appreciate language is important and has to be clear and concise but sometimes it gets ridiculous. My grandmother is the worst, but to be fair I don't see her very often as she lives miles away and only occasionally comes to stay for a holiday.

If I get a bit noisy she asks if I'll "go down for an hour" as if I'm a baby needing a sleep. I don't think she realises I'm fourteen and have never gone "down for an hour" even when I was a baby.

Actually, that's not strictly true.

When I was a baby, pre MMR, I slept normally. It's only since I haven't appeared to need much. Apparently when we flew back to UK from Brunei back in 1990, my mum was a bit concerned about me being awake on the long flight.

We were spending a few hours shopping in Singapore before catching the connecting flight to UK so the journey was extensive. Mum expressed her concerns to the sympathetic doctor in Brunei, and he gave her some medicine for me to take on the 'plane, which he assured her would knock an adult out within half an hour.

Thirty-six hours later, when we eventually arrived at Heathrow, it worked!

Until I was eight years old I didn't allow my mum to get much sleep either because I would be in her bed. Oh she tried to get me to stay in my own bed and would sit for hours with me holding my hand, waiting until I fell asleep, or she'd get in bed with me and gradually extricate herself from the bed in tiny movements over a long period of time.

It must have been really frustrating for her to go from lying comfortably next to me in the bed, to sliding over to the edge, slipping one leg on to the floor, then another, to kneeling down with her head still on the pillow and then, when she was sure I was sound asleep to very carefully get up and creep silently and stealthily out of the room, only to find that as soon as she got within two yards of the bedroom door, I would wake up.

She gave up in the end and I just slept in her bed.

She found this a bit confusing though because I didn't want to cuddle her at all, I just needed to know she was there.

I would throw out my arm or leg and provided I felt another human being I would sleep. Cuddly teddies and toys were no substitute and the only thing I would take to bed was a video box.

When my dad was home we used to play musical beds. Sometimes he would sleep with me in my parents' bed and mum would be in mine; and others, I would sleep with mum, and dad would be in my bed. This probably partly explains why I have no younger brothers or sisters.

However, it was my older brother who solved the problem. At the wise old age of ten, he suggested I was probably lonely and thought it would be a good idea if I slept in his room. At that time both Daryl and I had double beds and he thought I might just feel a bit lost and cold in mine.

Now Daryl has a big room but it was not large enough for two double beds so initially I slept with him in his bed. This was fine and I would lay quite a distance from him but close enough to check with my arm or leg that he was there.

Mum and dad were pleased because it finally meant they could have their own bed to themselves but were concerned I shouldn't get too used to sleeping with Daryl, as they knew as he got older, he wouldn't appreciate my presence.

They weren't sure how I'd react to being kicked out again though so they bought me a single bed and put that up alongside Daryl's double one. With a bit of maneuvering of furniture it fitted in well, and I stayed in his room for a while.

However, although I stayed in my bed, I didn't sleep all night long and when I was awake I chatted – a lot.

Needless to say this didn't go down too well with Daryl because my chattering wasn't something he could join in with.

It wasn't as though we indulged in brotherly conversations. I just used to burble away for hours and Daryl would stick his head under the covers and try to sleep. I'm surprised he didn't suffocate as he was under therc a long time.

One weekend when I went for respite care, my parents decorated my room in my favourite colour blue, and moved my bed back in.

They reasoned if I was able to sleep in a single bed on my own when I was at respite, there should be no problem with me doing the same at home.

They were right, and I've remained in my own bed, in my own room ever since, much to everyone's relief… especially Daryl's.

For Christmas last year, my parents bought me a new bed. It's a three quarter size one and they had it made three inches longer than normal because I've grown considerably in recent months. I'm taller than my mum now and almost as big as my brother.

I think my mum gets a bit embarrassed sometimes when we're out because if we're walking by a road she makes sure she's really close to me so I won't jump out in front of the traffic, and I often put my arm around her or hold her hand. I've heard her say people must think I'm her "toy boy".

She should be so lucky!

Now, I'm sure you've all heard about the strange rituals for which people with autism are renowned, but I don't actually have many now. However, I do have a sort of routine when I go to bed.

I usually go to bed sometime between nine and ten o'clock because even on weekends and school holidays I still get up early. There's no such thing as a lie-in at our house, except for my brother of course who's at the age where he could sleep all day.

My mum watched a programme on television once about teenagers. It said during puberty and adolescence there was a tremendous increase in brain activity so about eleven hours sleep was needed each night.

Unfortunately though, it's also the time when most teenagers want to stay up late, which explains why they're usually so grumpy and unsociable– not enough sleep.

A lot of parents seem to remark at a certain age they put their friendly young offspring to bed only to find when they get up the next morning they've turned into a different species who can't string sentences together and continually raise their eyes to the sky when asked to do something.

They also seem to become very clumsy, which is because their limbs grow so fast and that upsets their sense of balance.

I'm changing a bit I suppose because my sense of balance isn't what it used to be and I'm not quite so active these days. I'm not grumpy though, but then I've never really needed much sleep.

Ideally I like everyone else to go to bed when I do because of the noise factor but I'm not too bad now at letting people stay up if they have to.

In the past when we've had guests and it's been time for me to go to bed I've been known to give them their coats and open the front door.

Talk about a subtle hint!

Anyway, when it's bedtime I get a cup of water, go upstairs, turn the duvet on mum's bed back, put her television and bedside light on, go to the toilet, wash my hands, clean my teeth and put toothpaste on mum's toothbrush (I can't have her kissing me goodnight if her breath isn't fresh can I?)

I then rush into my room; half close the door and get in to bed pulling the covers up to my chin.

When my mum comes into the room, (breath smelling nice), I indicate I want her to pull the covers down at the foot of the bed.

Now I've told you my bed is three inches longer than normal so this used to be a problem, because although I had a double size duvet, if I pulled it up to my chin, it didn't overhang the bottom of the bed, and if I was satisfied with the bedding at the top, I was unhappy with the gap at the bottom.

The problem was resolved by getting me a king size duvet which now overhangs the sides and the bottom of my three quarter bed, which makes it lovely and cosy. Great!

When I'm happily tucked up in bed, my mum leans over me, gives me a kiss and says "Good night, sweet dreams, see you in the morning", which I repeat. If she forgets, I remind her by saying it first.

She then switches off the light and asks me if I want her to close the door. I always say, "Open", so she turns to leave and before she's walked halfway along the landing to the stairs, (a total distance of five of her steps), I've slammed the door.

I used to have to get out of my old bed to do it but with this new one ,which is slightly wider, I've discovered if I leave the door half open when I get into bed, all I have to do is sit up, reach out and give it a hard push.

Why do I do it? You tell me. Perhaps it's about having control.

Anyway, the door remains shut and I remain awake until everyone in the house is in bed and fast asleep.

Now if you didn't read my last book called, I'm not Naughty – I'm Autistic – Jodi's Journey – why not?

No it's all right, it's just when I finished the book I was hormonal and about to go into hospital to have a tooth out which was surplus to requirements. If you have a copy of my first book and look on the front cover you can actually see it at the top left of my mouth.

My brother hates that photograph of me. He says it doesn't look natural and of course it isn't. How many people do you know who just stand still against a wall and smile?

The one of mum on the back cover isn't any better even though she's not smiling, but in her defence she wasn't feeling very well at the time.

Anyway, mum was planning my tooth removal with military precision. She rang up the hospital and arranged with them that the day before my operation we should go in to look at the ward and have an explanation as to what would be happening.

At the same time the doctors were supposed to give me some cream so mum could put it on my hand at home the following morning, before I left for the hospital.

This would have allowed sufficient time to numb the area, so by the time I'd been documented, weighed, and had my blood pressure taken, I could be given the required anaesthetic and drift off to sleep.

The plan was good - it just didn't work.

You see the day before my operation was my birthday – thirteenth actually, and as there was no school, mum decided to take my brother and me ten pin bowling. The rink is in Ely, about five miles from where we live and in the same city as the hospital.

That sounds very grand doesn't it - city? Actually in terms of other cities in this country it's very small with the minimum amount of shops, etc. but does have a nice river and an absolutely wonderful, very famous cathedral, so warrants the title.

I love going in there – the echoes are amazing and if you stamp your feet on the marble floors the sound carries really well. I'm not so sure the other visitors to this marvelous building, which is well over a thousand years old, appreciate my sound effects though.

The last time I was in there was in January and in order to distract me from shouting my mum got my brother and I to follow the maze on the floor just inside the entrance to the cathedral.

If you follow it all the way round it's the equivalent of walking all the way up to the top of the tower and far less exhausting.

But now back to the bowling and mum booked a lane for 11 o'clock and we played for an hour. I did extremely well getting two strikes despite my rather unorthodox way of bowling.

I walk up to the line, hold the ball in both hands, and with legs astride, I bend my knees and roll it down the lane, usually very slowly. However, I am quite accurate and although sometimes it seems the ball will never get there, I do usually get some good scores.

I remember once though being taken to a tenpin bowling alley at an American airbase with a group of people from a local church group. Two of the members were volunteers in the Son-rise programme, which my mum was running for me at the time and so everyone was aware of my problem.

They knew my bowling wouldn't necessarily be like theirs but I think even they were surprised when my ball went so slowly it actually stopped.

I just walked up the lane, retrieved it and took another go. Many bowlers panicked because apparently it was dangerous. I didn't know that though as I have very little sense of danger, although it seems to be getting better.
Apparently, I might have been transported down the lane and scored a strike myself, but somehow I don't think I would have come back along the conveyor belt thing that returns the balls, do you?

After that, whenever it was my go, mum hovered about two feet behind me, arms at the ready, just in case!

Sorry, got a bit side-tracked there so back to my thirteenth birthday and my bowling treat. My brother won which really pleased him because he understands the concept of competition and when you do a sport or play a game the idea really is to win.

I couldn't care less as long as I enjoy myself. I'm not a bit competitive and am still coming to terms with the fact in tests the idea is to do as well as you can and thus impress people.

It's quite nice to hear "well done" and "good boy" though.

We rounded off the bowling session with a drink and some nice curly chips for lunch, and then headed off to the hospital.

It was closed. Well that's not strictly true. The hospital was open, but the ward we needed to visit and from where I was to obtain my cream was closed. It seems they'd got through that day's operations early and so had all left half an hour before we got there.

Mum hadn't actually arranged a time to call in at the ward and no one had thought to tell her it wouldn't be open all day.

Yet another example of how important clear communication is.

We hung around for a while deciding what to do and explained the situation to the nice receptionist and a passing doctor asked if he could help.

I bet he wished he hadn't because it took a lot longer than he'd anticipated and I expect he kept his surgery waiting.

However, he kindly took us up to the ward and let us peer through the window of the locked door so we would know where to go the following morning.

He said that if he could find the key and obtain permission from the dental staff at Cambridge he'd get us some of the cream we needed, as it wasn't dangerous and easy to use.

He even gave mum verbal instructions and a demonstration of how she should apply it, but it was all in vain.

He couldn't find the key, so he didn't get the cream, and we left empty handed with mum wondering how things would work out now her plans had been scuppered.

I should explain at this point that the Princess of Wales hospital is only used for day care and minor surgery now, although at one point it was a big RAF hospital.

Most of it has sadly now turned into a housing estate. Addenbrooke's which is the main hospital for the region is based in Cambridge, a very famous university city about twenty miles from where we live.

In order to make it easier for the patients from this area, teams of doctors, dentists and nurses travel to what's left of the hospital in Ely once or twice a week to perform minor surgery.

It makes life much simpler especially for those people for whom transport is an issue, and also, you don't have to pay to park at the hospital in Ely, which is a good thing. It's bad enough having to go for an operation or a hospital visit anyway without having to pay to park as well.

Still, there was no need to panic because prior to this hospital trip mum had been working on a strategy, which involved explanation and visual clues as to what would happen when I had my tooth out.

I had a video about a crocodile called Albert who had toothache and the fears he had about having his tooth removed. It ends when a kind dentist, removes the source of his pain from Albert's mouth, with the words "It's out Albert".

The crocodile hadn't felt a thing. It's a bit of a childish video I suppose, not at all age appropriate, but I was encouraged to watch it regularly prior to my hospital visit. I was also encouraged to look at the calendar and see that on 3rd April

2002, I was going to the hospital to have my tooth taken out by the dentist there.

The next part of mum's strategy was to do a bit of role-play. She mimed rubbing cream on my hand, giving me an injection, falling asleep, having my tooth pulled out, and then smiling.

This routine was accompanied with the words "Cream – injection – sleep – It's out Jodi". Then she added, "Okay?" for luck.

We went through this ritual often so when we turned up at the hospital I knew exactly what to expect. I soon held my hand out ready for the cream and was no trouble at all getting undressed or having my blood pressure taken.

The machine was really neat as I could see the numbers flash up before me, and it made a noise when it acquired the two figures required to confirm that my blood pressure was normal.

Mum discussed things with the dentist and anesthetists and it was agreed I could be first on the operation list, so about an hour and a half after I first arrived at the hospital, I walked, suitably attired, into the operation room. Mum came too with her hat, gown and plastic shoe covers on.

Once inside I was allowed to check out all the machines and look out of the window. They invited me to "hop onto the bed", (which is a bad expression to use on autists who do tend to take things literally). Fortunately, I knew what was expected of me though and so obliged by climbing up onto the bed.

I did make the mistake of trying to put my head on the pillow the wrong way though. Instead of lying on my back and resting the back of my head against it, I stuck my bum up in the air and put my forehead on it.

Hospital gowns are open at the back so I don't expect it was a pretty sight for the theatre nurse. Well, the instructions weren't very clear. I was just told to put my head on the pillow. No one told me which bit.

Anyway, they sorted me out and then I spotted the mask type machine, which I'd used on a previous occasion. Once before I'd had some baby teeth out and been given gas to send me to sleep.

I decided I must need it this time as well, so although the gas wasn't turned on, I took the mask, held it against my mouth and whilst I was attempting to breathe in the non-existent gas, the anaesthetist stuck the needle in my hand and that was it.

I went to sleep, snoring rhythmically.

My mum left the room and an hour later I was sitting up back in the ward complete with excess tooth in a little fairy envelope.

Actually it's well over an inch long and looks like a fang – not at all the type of thing you would put under the pillow for the fairies to collect. Mum has it in her jewellery box instead.

Apparently my grandmother had a similar high tooth removed from her mouth when she was a child, so I guess this genetic thing everyone talks about must account for something. She didn't have any anaesthetic at all though – brave thing.

I was wheeled back to the ward on my bed as I certainly couldn't walk back from the theatre and the sides were put up making it look as though I was in a cot.

It was a precautionary measure to make sure I didn't fall out as when I initially came round I was a bit disorientated. I knew I wanted to go home though and soon attempted to search for my clothes.

I had a drink of water and declared, "It's out" a few times, got dressed and wobbled about as I tried to make a quick exit.

However, there was no escape until I'd convinced everyone I wasn't going to be sick. Once I'd satisfied everyone on that score, mum was given instructions how to keep an eye on me for the next twenty-four hours and told to give me regular painkillers.

She was asked what we had in the medicine cupboard at home and what I would take, as they wanted to give me some straight away. Mum had good old Calpol but they recommended something stronger now I was a teenager, so I ambled over to the medicine cabinet and decided which painkiller I'd take.

I chose a nice orange flavoured one with a proper medicine spoon as opposed to those little plastic measuring cups you often get these days. I make it sound as though it was self-service which of course it wasn't. The nurse showed us the options and having tasted the Nurofen for children, the choice was easy.

I licked my lips with my tongue, told her it was "delicious" and then I was allowed home. The hospital rang up that afternoon and the following day just to check on me and said I had been "brilliant".

Mum had worried needlessly but is still adamant that preparation is vital. I think she's been watching too many DIY and gardening programmes personally, but have to admit that because of our little routine, I did know what to expect.

No truthfully, the more an autist is prepared for a situation the better. Some people make the mistake of thinking if a person doesn't speak, he or she has nothing to say, or worse, that they won't be able to understand things.

I don't say a lot although my vocabulary is increasing. I have a badge on my school bag, which says, "I'm more intelligent than people think" and I'm sure you'll find that's the case for most people with autism.

For instance when my mum decided I'd accumulated far too many videos in my room, she put some up into the attic. When she did so, she wisely showed and told me what she'd done so I wouldn't think they'd been sold or given away and want to replace them.

That used to get pretty expensive when I was younger and I know my mum still bears the mental scars of many horrible shopping excursions involving videos I didn't really need.

Now, though, whenever I decide I need to watch some of the videos in the attic, I type or write the titles out on a piece of paper and put "ladder" by the side of each.

Mum then gets the ladder out from the garage, (although I've been known to get it myself when she's been a bit slow on the uptake). I go up into the attic, retrieve the required videos and mum assists me down as I balance them all on one hand. She says I would make an excellent waiter.

If you read my first book, you may recall my mum was a bit concerned about how she'd be able to explain to me about not examining or fiddling with my private "bits" in public.

It's easy to explain to 'normal' kids. A family friend found her son looking at his penis in their lounge one day and demanded to know what he was doing. He was embarrassed, but replied as quick as a flash that he was "checking for lumps".

His mum told him to check for testicular cancer somewhere else, preferably in his bedroom or the bathroom, but my mum wasn't sure those instructions would work for me so she had to find another way.

My "play" room has a two way mirror in the door so mum is always able to see what I'm up to and she'd noticed me with my hands down my trousers, playing with myself, or studying my manhood as I watched a video.

She was a bit worried I might do a similar thing when I was out, or when there were other people around, so she sought the advice of my social worker who'd experienced this sort of thing before. Sheila came up with the idea of using picture cards – a method which had been tried and tested and had been quite successful in a number of cases.

The idea was there would be a sequence of pictures covering masturbation, showing where it is acceptable to do it and how.

You see not all people with special needs understand just what to do to achieve some sort of relief from the unusual sensations they're experiencing, and it's not the kind of thing you usually get someone to demonstrate to you personally either.

My brother is usually pretty good when mum says, "Just show Jodi how to ......" but somehow I don't think either of them wanted to try this one. We took Sheila's advice and had some pictures photocopied.

The first picture showed someone going into a bedroom. The next one was the person shutting the door, followed by him taking down his pants and trousers. He then sat on the bed and started to rub his erect penis.

The next picture was of him ejaculating, followed by a picture of him clearing up the mess with a tissue. He then got dressed, washed his hands and left the bedroom.

It's all clever stuff really and so sensible.

Obviously it can be used in all sorts of different situations and scenarios, and will change for boys and girls depending on the need for the pictures. Apparently the system is useful for girls when they start their periods.

Anyway, mum decided it might be a good idea to transpose my head onto the boys body in the photographs so I would realise it was supposed to be me. She planned also to take a photograph of my bedroom so that I would know where to go if I felt the urge to play with my "willy" as she put it.

Sheila also visited my respite care home to discuss having photographs taken of all the bedrooms there as well. This was because whenever I go to respite I sleep in different rooms, so if I got the urge to fiddle whilst I was over there I might get a bit confused as to where to go.

To date we've never used the photographs but it's a good idea don't you think?

At school we're also dealing with the subject in our “Boys” group and have so far watched a video, which deals with privacy in relation to growing up, and discussed it. Well, the rest of the group did. I was there, just didn’t contribute verbally.

Apparently there are various resources available to help reinforce the message about when and where it’s appropriate to touch one’s own body and remove clothing, etc.

My teacher is using words and symbols to reinforce this message, which apparently is so “important” and mum is getting involved too. I can’t see what all the fuss is about personally, but then I don’t get embarrassed, either for myself or other people.

Change of subject now.

A few weeks after my hospital date, I had another trip to the dentist. This time because of what my mum perceived to be toothache.

I'd been particularly noisy for some time especially at the dining table and more than intolerant towards my brother Daryl. I’d even hit him on a few occasions, which made him declare that he would “kill me”.

He didn’t mean it of course, but was justifiably annoyed at regularly being whacked very hard for no particular reason.

He did go through a phase of winding me up though by touching my hair every time he went past me, and he also took some chunks out of my hair a couple of times when he decided to cut out a solitary grey hair I had. Thank goodness he's not going to be a hairdresser when he leaves school as I ended up looking as though I had alopecia.

I'd also become more of an embarrassment to take out shopping, as I would suddenly scream at the top of my voice for seemingly no reason and without giving any warning. Anyway, on the Saturday before Easter, mum and I went to Tesco's, which was an unusually silly move on her part.

Picture the scene. The bank holiday is looming and the shops are going to be closed for one whole day so everyone is panic buying.

Wives have dragged their husbands and children out and trolleys are laden with goodies. Anyone would think the country was about to experience a famine. It's crowded and noisy particularly for anyone with sound sensitivity.

I was dutifully pushing our trolley very slowly and carefully, although I do confess to speeding up when mum removed her hand, which was restraining me a bit.

This wasn't a pleasant experience. Usually my mum takes me shopping when there aren't many people around and it's generally not noisy or crowded. I can then scoot down the aisles with one or both feet on the trolley if I want to.
Anyway, I spotted a clearing by the fruit and vegetable stand, sped over to it and stood and screamed out once at the top of my voice. This resulted in everyone jumping and a few people held their hands against the top of their chests.

I can never understand why people do that. It won't stop them having a heart attack.

Hushed silence followed and everyone turned to look in my direction, except of course for the woman who was retrieving her tomatoes from the floor where she'd dropped them and the couple who were apologising for bashing their trolley into the man in front.

It didn't bother me of course. I just looked across at my mum and said in a normal voice, "No shouting" as though she'd done it.

She looked me straight in the eye from where she was standing and replied in a kind but firm voice, "That's right Jodi – no shouting".

It's very important to make eye contact with people with autism but I think mum found it preferable on that occasion to look at me rather than at anyone else.

We just then carried on as if nothing had happened, but I did notice that we didn't buy any more shopping and she removed her hand from the trolley as we headed directly and speedily to the checkout.

My mum didn't really know what was wrong with me and put it down to hormones but then I kept saying things like "Ouch", "tooth", "hurt", "it's out" which were pretty good indicators that just maybe I had some dental problems.

Also, I was sleeping during the day, which was unheard of, so she rang my dentist to see if he could possibly examine me.

Unfortunately, my dentist was on holiday so Margaret, his receptionist, tried to book me into the dental unit at the hospital in Ely but they didn't have a clinic until the following week. She made several telephone calls and was finally able to get me an appointment with the community dentist in Cambridge.

I was told to turn up the next day as close to 10 o'clock as possible and they would fit me in. Margaret stayed late in the office arranging all this which mum said was service over and above the call of duty, so she bought her some flowers as a thank you.

Anyway, the next morning, my grandad drove mum, my brother and me to Cambridge for the simple reason mum was worried if I had any treatment I might need some comfort on the way home. She was concerned about being in the front seat driving whilst I was distracting her from the back of the car.

We arrived five minutes early and I was seen more or less straight away. The dentist and nurse were lovely as they had lots of experience of autism and for them I even lay down properly on the reclining seat so my teeth could be examined.

My regular dentist had never managed to get me to do that although he is really kind and gentle, so mum was pretty shocked.

The dentist told me I had beautiful teeth and none of them looked bad. She suggested I have an X-Ray and asked my mum whether I would oblige. As she's not really a mind reader, mum replied I might do if she demonstrated what was expected of me first, so that's exactly what happened.

Whilst mum put on the heavy safety apron, gripped the handrail and positioned herself so the machine could circle her head and take a photo, I stood with the dentist behind the screen watching. She explained to me what was happening and then told me it was my turn.

Suitably gowned, I stood still long enough to have a very clear X-ray taken whilst mum, also suitably gowned, stood by my side with her hand on my back, making encouraging remarks and telling me what a good boy I was.

The photo clearly revealed I was teething and was obviously in a lot of discomfort. The dentist said my second tooth was ready to burst through but my baby tooth was hanging on and there was very little room. She explained to my mum it was a bit like a baby teething only much worse.

She said the baby tooth would fall out eventually, but I'd previously been in a situation where two didn't and eventually I had to have them removed under anesthetic, hence my knowledge of the gas mask when I went into hospital.

The dentist said I had two choices. Either I could just leave it and let nature take its course in which case I should apply very strong teething gel to my gum and take some painkillers, or, she would take it out for me then and there.

As soon as I heard her mention "out" I went through the "cream-injection-sleep-it's out" routine so mum thought I might as well have it done, but then she was informed the dentist could only use local anaesthetic.

This would have meant sticking needles in either side of the tooth to be removed in order to numb the area, but I'd be conscious of the whole operation.

Mum decided the risks just weren't worth it. For the first time in my life I'd actually laid on a dental chair and had my teeth examined properly so she didn't want to do anything to frighten me, cause me pain and put me off visiting the dentist in the future.

The dentist also explained if mum did decide for the latter and I struggled, she would discontinue the process, so I might have gone through a bad experience for nothing.

Mum decided to let nature take its course and a week later my tooth was out and my temperament improved.

Mum felt able to take me shopping again.

Daryl, my brother, went through a phase where he kept getting headaches and said his eyes kept going funny. My mum picked up on this because she noticed he had some work in his schoolbook, which wasn't in his handwriting.

When she questioned him about it, he said someone else had written it for him because he (Daryl) couldn't see the board.

Mum booked an appointment at the opticians for the following Saturday morning and he presented himself for his examination at the required time.

Mum signed the form for him, as he was still a minor and decided it might be wiser to take me shopping rather than sit and wait in a room full of expensive spectacles and frames, although I did quite enjoy looking at myself in all the mirrors they had in the room.

She arranged to meet him back at the opticians in twenty minutes, and we went next door to Woolworths.

Yes, I know in my first book, after a particularly bad experience in the shop with me, mum declared she'd buy a long blonde wig and never set foot inside the door again, but time is a great healer. Besides she was losing her memory.

More on that later though.

Daryl actually works there at weekends now so I guess his bad memories about the store have also healed.

True to form I headed for the video section and managed to find another title to add to my collection. Mum had no objection to me having it and we went up to the counter with the empty box so that I could get the actual video and pay.

Whilst we were waiting I said "Fun Time Favourites". Mum asked me to repeat it, so I obliged.

She looked and couldn't see anything so she asked the shop assistant whether they had a video called "Fun Time Favourites" and explained that it was a Thomas the Tank Engine one.

An autistic friend of mine had borrowed it from the library once when I had been to visit him and although it contained episodes that I already had on my vast collection of other Thomas videos, I wanted it.

The assistant said she didn't think they had it and had never heard of it so I elaborated a bit and said, "I want Fun Time Favourites, please".

This time my mum followed my gaze to the bottom shelf behind the counter where there were lots of black videotapes standing on their ends. They all looked identical except for the labels that you had to tilt your head at an angle of ninety degrees to read.

Sure enough, there on the bottom shelf partly hidden by a cardboard box was the video I'd been searching for at every car boot sale for weeks. Mum was so astounded she bought me that one too and I happily returned to the opticians to find Daryl waiting patiently for us.

His eyes had changed a bit but not sufficiently for him to need glasses.

When mum recounted the Woolworths video story to her friend Jane, who happens to be the mother of the autistic boy I've just mentioned, she remarked that I was "incredible".

Jane says I'm like one of those half men, half machine, people you see in movies with their X-ray vision. I do seem to be able to tune into some things much faster than everyone else but then maybe they just don't like Thomas the Tank Engine as much as I still do.

Mum read an article once about why autistic children seem to like Thomas and his friends so much, and apparently it's because the faces of the engines, etc., are so big and expressive.

Also, in the stories it's only the big main characters that move whilst the background remains still so it's less confusing for us.

When my first book was published there was quite a lot of local interest and things changed yet again for me when my photo appeared on the front of our local paper.

That evening my mum was sitting quietly in the kitchen having a well-deserved cup of tea when she received a telephone call from a strange lady.

Actually she's not at all strange but mum had never met or even heard of her before and her first question after the initial introduction of, "Hello, I've been following your story on the radio and in the newspapers" was, had mum had ever considered I might not be autistic?

That was a weird question considering the reason why the photo was in the paper in the first place was because my book had just been published clearly entitled, "I'm not Naughty – I'm Autistic – Jodi's Journey", and my mum, my brother, and I were posing beautifully to promote it.

That would hardly suggest anyone thought me anything other than autistic.

My mum is very polite though and talks to anyone – even in waiting rooms at the doctor and dental surgeries.

She always tries to see the best in people.

My dad and brother are always asking how she knows the person she has just spent the last few minutes chatting to, or greeted in the street.

Invariably she doesn't know them at all and dad often tells her off for speaking to strangers especially if they are men, but she says it costs nothing to be nice to people.

She says also that she remembers vividly all the times she felt so alone and desperate for conversation when I was the toddler from hell.

No one ever came to visit us when I was little except social workers and my grand parents. Mum spent most of her life talking to the walls so I suppose that memory helps.

Unsurprisingly therefore, she asked the obvious question "Why?" and thus began the conversation that changed her life and mine.

Pam, the lady on the 'phone, suggested I could be mercury poisoned. Actually, the correct term is "mercury toxic" as it seems the powers that be don't like the word "poison" very much.

Wonder why?

It seemed it had something to do with teeth, not mine but my mums.

Anyway, mum chatted for a while and arranged to visit this lady and her husband at their home to find out more. What she was to discover was very interesting and because the sharing of knowledge makes you immortal, I'm going to let her pass it on to you.

Right, are you sitting comfortably? Then I'll hand you over to my mum and I'll be back later.

Jean - 1

Okay, well as I'm now in control of the story I apologise for appearing to be getting off the track of autism, but I assure you it's all relevant. Just think of it as taking the scenic route.

One of the hardest things for me, as a mother, has been the feeling of guilt concerning Jodi's autism. I have always asked "Why?"

I've never found an answer, and whilst accepting he's autistic made life so much easier, it never made the feeling of uncertainty about whether it was something I'd done or hadn't done go away. I think, as is the case in most situations, you can accept anything if you understand why it happened.

I believe I now know why my beautiful son is autistic and whilst it won't help him recover – if that's the right word it's certainly put my mind to rest somewhat that it wasn't my fault.

I may be completely wrong. You'll have to decide for yourself.

Pam, the instigator of the strange telephone call said she felt compelled to telephone me because circumstances in her own life had given her knowledge which might just help me.

Later she also confessed that she'd thought I was ill because my eyes looked "dead". I have to say I was a bit put out about that actually because I'd considered the photograph in the newspaper was quite good and that I'd looked, dare I say it, quite “passable”. Just goes to show you never see yourself the way others do.

During the course of the telephone conversation and the subsequent meeting I discovered that Pam’s husband had been extremely ill to the point that when everyone else was celebrating the eve of the year 2000, Bryan was on his hands and knees thanking God he was still alive to see it.

I'll now relay his story because it’s not only interesting, but also helps explain why I took the course of action I did with Jodi.

Bryan had been a radiographer in the RAF and has the distinction of holding the Diploma Society of Radiographers (Diagnostic), which I’m told is quite rare, so, “Well done, Bryan”.

When he was sixty though, Bryan began to display weird psychological symptoms. He had personality changes, couldn’t relax, became agitated, impulsive and acted completely out of character.

In 1999, Pam found him collapsed in the garden and Bryan was diagnosed as having had a stroke. Later, he was diagnosed with having had a further one and his symptoms began to intensify.

His short-term memory was dreadful; he was indifferent to everything, depressed and often talked of suicide.

Bryan began to avoid social situations and didn’t care about the general running of his home, either financially or physically.

He was confused, couldn't work out minor problems or even remember how to turn on his computer, which he loved. The poor man also developed physical symptoms like tremors in his hands and spasms in his arms and legs.

Often when he walked across the room his legs would just seize up or sometimes give way and he'd find himself in a heap on the floor. He became very dizzy and had balance problems with ataxia which is the inability to co-ordinate the muscles.

Poor Bryan!

He was getting really desperate and his symptoms appeared to be a combination of strokes, dementia, Alzheimer's disease, Parkinson's and Multiple Sclerosis.

There was no specific diagnosis initially – just a whole load of worrying symptoms and no answers.

Pam is a Registered General Nurse and has worked in several care homes. She's had many years' experience working "hands on" with people diagnosed with all the conditions being suggested for her husband.

Many of her patients have died, though I hasten to add that it has nothing to do with her competence as a nurse. She felt her husband was heading the same way and was desperate to find a cure.

She used to have to lock him in the house when she went to work each night and never knew what she would find upon her return, but someone had to pay the bills.

Bryan couldn't.

The strain must have been tremendous.

In July 2000, when Bryan felt he was dying, and Pam didn't want to begin the new century as a widow, she clutched at the only straw offered to her at that time, which was a suggestion Bryan had made that he might have mercury poisoning from his dental amalgam.

Apparently he'd read about it somewhere many months earlier and been dismissed by not only Pam but also by GP's and consultants including a consultant neurologist.

In desperation Pam sought out the yellow pages and found a Natural Health Practitioner who specialised in clinical treatments based on biochemistry, nutrition and toxicology.

His name was Chris Mascarenhas of Highway Health Practice.

She phoned him up and begged him to see Bryan. Chris agreed and told them to come straight over.

Somehow Pam managed to get Bryan into the car but it took both her and Chris to get him into the clinic despite him having a walking stick.

By this time he had tinnitus, persistent nausea, headaches and was sensitive to light. His right leg shook so much he couldn't walk on it and his left leg was almost as bad. Both arms and hands also shook visibly, and Bryan couldn't stand unaided.

Things weren't looking good.

Chris looked inside Bryan's mouth and saw several amalgam fillings as well as a gold crown.

Chris performed an Electro Dermal Screening test on Bryan. This is a non-invasive screening protocol, which identifies toxins and imbalances within the body.

It was very evident Bryan was incredibly ill, but the test revealed the reason as he had high levels of mercury, aluminium, lead and chromium in his body.

Chris recommended Bryan immediately started a de-toxification programme and have his fillings removed, as the key component in amalgam fillings is mercury.

He had to use a roborating chelator, which removes the organic based heavy metals from the body whilst at the same time replacing them with vital minerals.

There's no question in Pam's mind this, combined with the removal of his fillings, saved Bryan's life.

Having the amalgam removed from his mouth was obviously crucial but it should be done properly otherwise there could be all sorts of problems.

Ideally you should do it half way through a de-toxification programme, using a clean rubber dam for each filling to ensure there's no cross contamination, and you should wear an oxygen mask so you don't breathe in the mercury vapour.

I'll explain why later, but Bryan didn't do any of that. There was no time - he was too ill.

Pam persuaded her dentist, Doug Vincent, to remove all Bryan's visible fillings the next day, so he opened up his surgery especially for them one Saturday afternoon.

No rubber dams were used but Bryan had started his de-tox.

Thankfully, he began to improve and it appeared all was well. However, two weeks after finishing the de-tox all his symptoms returned.

Bryan went back to see Chris and the test revealed he still had high levels of mercury and chromium, so back he went to the dentist.

It was discovered the gold crown Bryan had in his mouth, was covering an amalgam filling and the two metals were reacting with each other.

They were infact creating a battery effect. Each time Bryan touched his crown he received an electric shock and that was worsening his serious neurological problems.

Pam and Bryan have now reported the potential dangers of mercury toxicity when a gold crown is placed over amalgam to the Medical Devices Agency as an adverse incident.

Strangely, amalgam is considered a medical device and that's where the problem lies when things go wrong.

When people suffer worrying health symptoms they naturally report to the doctor rather than to the dentist, so the different authorities don't tie up the relevant information.

It's particularly difficult especially as symptoms can appear up to five years after dental work has been carried out, so it's not surprising there's a widespread disbelief, amalgam fillings can be dangerous for some people..

Anyway, Bryan had his gold crown removed and took it home. He put it in water and said it was incredible the amount of bubbles that came out of it, because of the mercury vapour.

It seems when you have amalgam with another metal you get up to 60% more mercury vapour than normal.

Frightening stuff!

With the gold crown out of his mouth, Bryan continued to improve, and if you saw him today it would be hard to believe he'd ever been so ill. He's just decorated his house. Can you imagine him trying to do that when his limbs were shaking uncontrollably?

I suppose at this point I should explain all about amalgam dental fillings so you know what all the fuss is about.

Dental amalgam has been used to fill dental cavities for well over 150 years and apart from those incredibly lucky people who've never had a filling, or those unlucky people who have dentures; most people will have one or two.

They are those grey fillings, which start off all smooth and shiny. Have you ever considered how they're made or what's in them? I certainly hadn't until I discovered they were most likely the cause of my weird health symptoms.

Amalgam actually means a mixture of mercury and another metal or in this case metals, and amalgam fillings are now made up of 50% mercury and the remaining 50% comprises a mixture of silver, tin, copper, and sometimes zinc in uneven proportions.

The composition varies with each manufacturer and seemingly the higher the copper content the more dangerous it is.

These metals are all bound together with liquid mercury, which then hardens. The amalgam (mercury/metal mixture) is then put in your mouth to plug the holes in your teeth and should solve your teething problems.

Lucky old you – well, maybe not.

It could just be causing all sorts of health problems and perhaps those people with dentures are the lucky ones after all!

I don't know whether you're an expert in science or not. I'm certainly not but I do know when various metals get put together they can react in different ways.

Metals corrode especially when they're exposed to moisture so it really makes you wonder what possessed someone to decide to put these toxic ones in our mouths.

Did they forget about the constant supply of saliva and the regular supply of various other liquids?

Anyway, when the different metals in dental amalgam deteriorate, electrochemical reactions in the saliva can create weak electric currents, so your mouth can become a bit like a battery.

The electrical currents discharged from fillings follow the path of least resistance apparently, which is into the body and up to the brain.

I had seven amalgam fillings in my mouth and got to the stage where I couldn't talk on the telephone because it made me feel sick, dizzy and disorientated. My head would feel hot and I'd also get a red patch on my left cheek.

It felt as though it was burning and numb at the same time, and my left eye felt as if it was being dragged down.

I felt certain if I looked in the mirror my face would be distorted, but it never was.

Everyone thought I was mad when I told them how I felt but the only way I could have a conversation with anyone over the telephone was if I spoke through the speaker system and stayed well back.

Even then the conversations had to be short.

I couldn't use my mobile phone at all so it's just as well my service provider wasn't relying on my calls to make a profit. Sitting at the computer also made me feel distinctly ill.

Okay, you might say, that's all very well but I thought those metals were encased in mercury which is really hard and you would be right. The problem is amalgam fillings get worn away over time with chewing, brushing and corrosion.

Mercury is the second most toxic metal on the planet, the first one being plutonium. You probably know Egyptians used mercury to repel tomb raiders because it is so dangerous and warnings are always given not to breathe it in or ingest it.

Do you remember the Mad Hatter in Alice in Wonderland? Ever wondered where his character came from?

Well. Mercury used to be used in the hat making process and many people went mad, so Mercury toxicity, the preferred title, is often referred to as Mad Hatter's Disease.

Now back to teeth and more information.

Mercury is the only metal that evaporates at room temperature, and if you have any amalgam fillings it's in your mouth.

One large filling apparently contains more mercury than you'd find in a thermometer, so it doesn't take a brain surgeon to work out if you have even one amalgam filling you're going to get some mercury vapour.

It's being released all the time, but when you chew or drink hot liquids you get even more. Seemingly, it takes at least an hour before the increased release of mercury stops after chewing, so if you have any amalgam fillings and are one of these people who grind their teeth, chew gum, snack or drink coffee all day long, you might just want to revise your eating habits.

I used to drink loads of cups of tea and coffee during the day and couldn't understand why I would suddenly come over so tired that I couldn't keep my eyes open.

My head would feel incredibly heavy and would drop to my chest as though my neck had given way and although I would fight to stay awake, there was nothing I could do to stop my eyelids from closing.

I never dare drive in the afternoon because between two and three o'clock were the worst periods. I generally ate lunch at one o'clock.

There's some speculation many road accidents could be a result of a mercury toxic person falling asleep at the wheel after a meal.

After my recent experience, I can well believe it. It was pretty embarrassing when I did sleep though as I used to dribble and whatever I lay my head on got soaked.

At night when I went to bed I slept in an upright position propped up with lots of pillows because not only did I salivate a lot, but also I used to stop breathing when I lay flat. It was as though my nostrils closed up, my throat was blocked and no air could get through.

I'd find myself being jerked awake, which must have resembled someone who'd had a heart attack being shocked back to life. It was very frightening.

Now I sleep horizontally with just one pillow and I certainly don't dribble.

In 1997, the British Dental Association estimated three percent of the population suffered from mercury sensitivity. I don't know how many people were in the UK then, but in July 2001 there were estimated to be 59,647,790.

My maths are about as good as my science so if I round it up to 60,000,000 it makes explanations a lot easier and three percent of that figure is 1.8 million.

That's a lot of people.

If you're not in the minority of the population affected by amalgams, then the mercury vapour should pass through the skin in your mouth into your blood stream. You can then get rid of it through your urine or by breathing it out to share with everyone else.

How generous!

It seems just as you can inhale other people's smoke, the same thing can apply to mercury vapour. Talking to someone face to face, especially if they've just had dental work done or recently had a hot drink or meal could be a problem.

Maybe people with autism have it right when they look in the opposite direction, after all.

According to articles, which appeared in certain newspapers and women's magazines, the Queen of England advised the late Princess Diana to have her amalgam fillings removed as far back as 1989 for health reasons.

It makes you wonder if she took her advice considering all the problems the poor lady had prior to her untimely death.

Anyway, mercury usually only stays in your bloodstream for a short transit period and then you either urinate or excrete it away. That's if you're one of the ninety seven percent of the population who supposedly don't have a problem.

Lucky you!

For those who fall into the sensitive category though, the story doesn't have a happy ending. It begins the same with the mercury vapour getting into the blood stream, but instead of leaving, it attaches itself to the fatty tissues in the body.

You see mercury is what's known as a fat binding toxin so it makes a bee line for places like your kidneys, liver, pancreas and brain, which makes it very difficult to test for.

If you go along to your GP and suggest you might have mercury toxicity caused by your amalgam fillings in your mouth it's unlikely you'll be taken seriously.

ECG's and X-Rays won't reveal anything and neither will blood tests unless you have them done whilst the mercury is still in the blood stream and it's highly unlikely you'll do that if you suffer from mercury poisoning caused by your dental amalgams.

You could of course have a biopsy done but the problem there would be knowing which organ to choose?

Undoubtedly you're now asking, "If amalgam is potentially so dangerous why are dentists still using it?"

Right?

I did, and apparently there are a few reasons.

The first is obviously because it's been used for well over 150 years and in all honesty there isn't anything to replace it in terms of cost and durability.

In 1812, Joseph Bell developed the forerunner of modern amalgam. He was a British chemist, and his filling was made from a paste formed out of filings from silver coins and mercury.

The impurities in the coins caused problems though because the mixture expanded and cracked the teeth.

Clearly the composition had to change.

Amalgam was originally developed as a cheaper alternative to gold for fillings but there have been questions about its safety ever since.

Did you know there's been what's come to be known as the Amalgam Wars?

It seems those that favoured amalgam accused the gold camp of being money grabbers and denying the majority of the population the opportunity of having their teeth filled, and the gold camp in return argued mercury was poisonous.

Anyway, it was introduced to UK in 1819 and USA in the late 1820's. It's been around ever since and there lies the problem.

You see way back in the 1800's there were no safety regulatory bodies. By the time safety testing began amalgam had been on the scene for many years. As a result the powers that be considered it must be safe so it was "grand-fathered" in and is still here.

There was a resolution passed in America in 1845 'pronouncing the use of amalgams as malpractice', but many dentists defied the ban because it was inexpensive, easy to use, durable and had no apparent side effects.

Dentists have always disputed its safety but it appears to have become the filling of choice for financial reasons. Even today, despite all the evidence to the contrary, most dentists support the argument mercury is locked into the fillings and can't escape.

It would be hard for dental authorities to advise patients of the possible side effects to some people without implying it could potentially be dangerous.

Also the alternatives are comparatively new, so the long-term side effects of those are still in doubt. The answer clearly is to look after your own teeth and hope you never need a filling.

Amalgam is unquestionably incredibly durable and will probably outlast you, especially if you're one of those people who have difficulty in getting rid of the mercury.

It won't actually kill you itself but it can play havoc with your central nervous and immune systems, making you vulnerable to all sorts of things.

It's not the cause of all illnesses but there's a lot of speculation it's most likely a contributory factor in many because it accumulates in tissues and organs.

Some dentists will offer a non-amalgam white filling, but they charge more for it and that puts a lot of people off. You see it will probably be a composite, which is usually made of ground glass powder mixed with a plastic binder.

The filling has to be done gradually by building up composite layers and each one has to be cured by means of having a blue fibre optic light applied to it before the next layer can be put on.

It's a time consuming process and difficult to perform, as the tooth has to be really dry so the composite can be bonded onto the tooth.

Ideally, each composite should be done using a rubber dam. Composites tend to only last a few years, and they're also difficult to shape to get a nice finish.

If you don't get a really good seal there's the risk of infections as the composites shrink, and they aren't suitable for everyone.

The other alternative to amalgam of course is gold, which is expensive and is quite soft in its pure state, so other metals are added. That makes it more durable and cheaper.

Gold is however another metal in your mouth and can, I'm told, cause depression. It's also been known to set off metal detector alarms at airports, so unless you particularly like being frisked, it might be one to avoid.

Also, as you're unlikely to have pure gold in your mouth, the mixture of the metals could generate an electrical current, which will be discharged into the mouth and to the brain.

The second reason amalgam is still used (in UK at least), is because there's currently a national shortage of dentists even to perform the normal work needing to be done.

Many people can't find a National Health Dentist (NHS) as it is and whenever a new practice opens there are queues of people trying to register.

Just imagine the chaos if everyone with amalgam fillings decided they wanted them removed and replaced with alternatives. It would be an impossible task and economically disastrous.

The third reason why amalgam is being used is because it's currently government policy to do so. Countries like Norway and Sweden are much more enlightened and have already realised the potential danger of mercury.

Their health authorities recommend dentists no longer use amalgam on their patients.

Amalgam technology is no longer taught in Swiss dental schools and many governments throughout the world have introduced restrictions on its use, not only for pregnant and nursing mothers, but also in children and people with kidney and nervous system disorders.

In USA where people sue for just about anything, (probably because that's where most of the world's lawyers are), there are precautions in place to avoid litigation.

Since July, 2002, dentists in Maine have had to display a poster in the public waiting area of their surgeries and provide each patient with a copy of a brochure explaining the potential advantages and disadvantages to oral health, overall human health and the environment of using mercury or mercury amalgam in dental procedures.

That's not really surprising though because it seems dentists (in the USA anyway) were given recommendations of Mercury Hygiene as far back as the 1980's for their protection against mercury and scrap amalgam. That's the bit left over after a filling has been placed.

These fifteen regulations documented by the Council on Dental Materials and Devices included - working in well-ventilated spaces, avoiding heating mercury or amalgam, using a no–touch technique for handling the amalgam, storing mercury in unbreakable, tightly sealed containers, alerting all personnel of the potential hazard of mercury vapour, and getting anyone regularly employed in a dental office to have an annual mercury check up.

Seemingly the scrap amalgam was considered dangerous to dentists and yet the amalgam placed in the filling was considered safe.

Doesn't that seem strange to you?

Obviously the lawyers (in Maine at least) have now decided it's time for the patients to be alerted and advised too.

I wonder if that will ever happen in UK?

The British Dental Association (BDA) have issued statements on the safety of amalgam advising dentists amalgam fillings are free from risk of systemic toxicity and are not a threat to general health.

They admit very occasionally, people experience a local sensitivity reaction but this can be sorted by removing the filling.

It appears in America at one stage, dentists faced being struck off if they so much as hinted amalgam might be a contentious issue. I can understand that.

After all, if your employers tell you something is okay, they wouldn't take too kindly to you advising people otherwise and I don't suppose there's much call for a dentist without a licence.

The BDA also recommended where clinically reasonable, amalgam fillings shouldn't be placed or replaced during pregnancy. They said the advice suggested by The Department of Health was given as a precaution and not because of any evidence of harm to the baby's development or health.

You'll be pleased to learn amalgam is no longer used on pregnant women or children in some practices in the UK so the precautionary advice had some effect obviously.

Some dentists, have seen first hand the problems dental amalgam can cause and the benefits to the patient once it's been safely removed.

The dentist who so kindly opened up his surgery and removed Bryan's amalgam fillings and later, his gold crown, now runs a completely Mercury Free Dentistry practice in Ely. It's called Newnham Dental Practice and Dr. D.R. Vincent BDS (London), or Doug as he's known, is the man to see.

He now uses the rubber dam and ensures the patient is on a de-toxification programme for a minimum of two weeks before he'll start treatment to remove and replace amalgam fillings, because he knows it can be dangerous.

Good for him that's what I say.

Now, I'm sure you're wondering what Bryan's teeth have to do with Jodi and the answer is absolutely nothing. However, mine do.

You see for the past four years at least I hadn't been feeling "quite right". I'd been to the doctors on a few occasions but they could never find anything wrong so of course whenever anyone asked me how I was, I always responded with "great, thanks", or "fine".

That's one thing an autist would never do – lie. They tell it how it is.

However, I didn't want to sound like a hypochondriac and outwardly I generally looked okay. It's amazing what a bit of lipstick and eye shadow can do. If I was a bit pale I'd just rub some colour into my cheeks and everyone thought I looked really well "considering".

I assume they were referring to Jodi, and the fact Malcolm is away so much. He, as you might remember, works abroad most of the time, but he is my rock and a big part of this family.

People are always telling me how well I cope but I don't know any different.

I hate going to the doctors, not because I don't like them personally, but it just seems such a waste of my time. I rarely see the same doctor as where we live there's a Health Surgery with lots of general practitioners (GP's).

Our village is expanding rapidly and they've built a new, larger surgery to cope with the demand. The problem at the moment though is finding sufficient, qualified doctors to staff it.

The most senior practice doctor who'd been here for years retired and they had difficulty finding anyone to replace him. It appears there's a chronic shortage of NHS doctors, just as there's a shortage of dentists.

Consequently, the wonderful doctors we have are really busy and people quip you have to know you're going to be ill a week in advance just to get an appointment!

Anyway, once I decided I really ought to see someone about the increasing amount of weird symptoms I was developing, I took the first appointment offered, with whomever it was offered. On occasions I've seen a visiting locum and perhaps that's where I went wrong.

Now I'm not saying that the locums or any of the doctors were incompetent, far from it, but they're all restricted to a few minutes surgery time. I think it's something like seven minutes. If you always see a different doctor and time is crucial, it's possibly difficult to pinpoint exactly what's going on.

I had great faith in them though – all of them and still do. They have my utmost admiration, as it can't be easy for general practitioners. There are so many different problems and everyone wants an immediate diagnosis and a cure.

I saved up my visits to the doctor and would list my ailments until I had a sufficient amount to warrant my seven minutes of the doctor's valuable time.

At first they were just written on bits of paper, which I'd memorise in the waiting room before I went in, but gradually the list got longer so I had to read it out.

By the time I'd received the telephone call from Pam, I required a whole piece of A4 typed paper so I just handed over a copy directly to the doctor. It saved time and also by then I could barely remember why I went from one room to another so I never would have remembered all my symptoms anyway.

I used to stick notes up all over the place reminding me to do things.

Daryl jokingly declared I was "losing it".

Unfortunately he was right. My short-term memory was deplorable.

Now all the doctors were brilliant. They checked my blood pressure, heartbeat, and took blood and urine samples. I had two electro-cardiograms and an X-ray and all sorts of tests were done but nothing ever showed up.

I had it in my mind I might be pre-menopausal because I was forty-seven at that stage and the age seemed about right. I'd had a hysterectomy done about six years earlier so no longer had the periods that might have confirmed my suspicions, but I still have my ovaries.

The doctors couldn't find anything wrong with me and suggested I could be stressed. Funny that. There seems to be a general consensus of opinion if you have an autistic child you must be stressed, so I suppose in a veiled sort of way, Jodi was being made a scapegoat for my situation.

I knew there was something else going on though and the only stress I had was not knowing what. I knew Jodi wasn't to blame and if you've read the first book you'll know he's much easier to live with now.

When he was about four and really difficult I almost had a breakdown. Now that was stress, but even then Jodi wasn't entirely to blame.

At the time my husband was away, Daryl, my eldest son, had just started primary school and I had to ferry him backwards and forwards to school.

I'd also just finished supervising the building of our new house, which included organising all the workmen and ordering every single screw, brick, tile, etc., as well as doing as many labour type jobs as I could, and I have to admit to feeling really proud of that achievement.

Anyway, we'd just moved in and I was also working as a courier to deliver parcels, as well as trying to comprehend and look after Jodi who was completely baffling and incredibly demanding.

When Malcolm came home and I was able to relax a bit, I just lost it. The doctor had to be called out to me because I couldn't get out of bed.

He examined me, asked a few questions and declared, "My dear girl, you're exhausted". Well, actually he didn't say, "exhausted", he used another nine-letter word usually associated with horses and it begins with "kn", but you get the idea.

How are you enjoying the scenic tour? Are you still with me?

Anyway, back to the story I was actually attempting to tell, which brings us back to the telephone call from Pam.

After I'd listened to Bryan's story I checked up on the symptoms of mercury toxicity from dental amalgams.

There were several sources of information on the internet, all pretty much saying the same thing, and I found to my horror every single item on the latest A4 sheet I'd called my "I think I'm a hypochondriac" file appeared. It was almost as though I had written the symptoms myself.

I felt excited, frightened and sick.

In case you're interested I'll tell you what you can find about the Signs and Symptoms of Mercury Vapour Exposure from Mercury Amalgam Dental Fillings found at www.curezone.com/dental/mercury_symptoms.html, but if you type "dental amalgam and mercury" in any search engine you'll come up with similar results.

Another good point of reference, which I highly recommend is a book by Dr. Hal A. Huggins, entitled, "It's All In Your Head".

Basically, the first symptoms are vague psychic ones and your short-term memory deteriorates (Tell me about it!).

It's hard to concentrate on anything, which requires attention, or thinking and you prefer not to learn anything new.

You avoid social contact and have mood swings, often losing your temper for seemingly no reason.

You become physically exhausted and clumsy because it is hard to co-ordinate your movements with your visual impressions (ataxia).

You get occasional headaches and minor involuntary muscle spasms and ticks.

Your hands and feet get cold easily and sometimes you can't focus your eyes clearly.

Also you can get vertigo and dizziness attacks.

At an early stage you often get joint and muscle pains, stiffness, and lumbago.

You get an irregular heartbeat and pulse, which makes you feel anxious, and you don't sleep well so wake up feeling stiff and never thoroughly rested.

You are constantly tired.

Some people develop irritable bowel syndrome and bloating is common.

Some people develop sinusitis and the upper respiratory tract can easily become chronically inflamed.

Many people suffer from mouth disorders, bleeding gums, blisters, aching teeth and jaws, and a metal taste in the mouth is a direct sign of metal poisoning (mercury, copper).

The more poisoned you are, the more serious the problems can become and the pituitary and thyroid glands can be affected.

Neurological symptoms such as numbness, hypersensitivity and paralysis can worsen so all in all it's not very nice.

Okay, how many of you are rubbing your tongue over your teeth and thinking "I've got a metal taste in my mouth"?

A lot, I'll bet.

If you want a quick check as to some, though probably not all of the symptoms associated with amalgam fillings then read on as I've listed them under some specific headings.

These aren't my words but come from many reputable sites on the web.

* Immunological – allergies, asthma, rhinitis, sinusitis, swollen lymph nodes in neck

* Endocrine – subnormal temperature, cold clammy hands and feet, excessive perspiration, muscle weakness, fatigue, hypoxia, oedema, loss of appetite, loss of weight, joint pain.

* Psychological Disturbances - irritability, nervousness, fits of anger, memory loss, lack of attention, depression, low self-confidence, anxiety, drowsiness, shyness/timidity, decline of intellect, insomnia, and low self-control.

* Oral Cavity Disorders – bleeding gums, white patches in mouth, stomatitis, bone loss around teeth, loosening of teeth, ulcers of gums – palate – tongue, excessive saliva, burning of mouth, foul breath, gum pigmentation, metallic taste.

* Gastrointestinal Effects – abdominal cramps, colitis, Crohn's disease, gastrointestinal problems, diarrhoea.

* Systemic Effects – cardiovascular, irregular heart beat, changes in blood pressure, feeble or irregular pulse, pain or pressure in chest.

* Neurological – chronic or frequent headaches, dizziness, ringing or noises in ears, fine tremors (hands, feet, eye lids, tongue).

* Respiratory – persistent cough, emphysema, shallow or irregular breathing

That's quite a list isn't it and I had several of them. I'd reached the point where apart from the other symptoms I've mentioned, I felt out of breath just walking upstairs, my right leg had given way a few times, I often felt as though I was walking on a rocking boat and my hand had shaken so badly that I couldn't even thread a piece of cotton through the hole of a wool needle.

I used to fumble when I washed up or hung the washing out and I had inexplicable pains, aching joints, leg cramps, ringing noises in my ears and frequent heartburn. My left eyelid used to flicker and I also developed irritable bowel syndrome.

I was filled with a mixture of emotions – relief because I finally felt I knew what was wrong with me, and fear because I realised unless I did something about it, things could only get worse.

I was terrified about what would happen to my children if I became too ill to look after them and of course I did think about death.

That's one of the things that really worry me about Jodi. I fear for what will happen to him when I'm gone. I know no one would be willing and able to look after him the way I can, at the moment at least.

I understand him better than anyone and tolerate far more than anyone else would, which may not always be a good thing, but that's just how mums are.

I'm going to a seminar organised by The Royal MENCAP Society soon to make sure the provisions we've made for him in our wills will give him the security he'll need in the future. That's such an important consideration.

Anyway, I told my parents about the telephone conversation, my meeting with Pam and Bryan, and my subsequent discoveries about mercury toxicity over a tearful cup of tea in their kitchen.

Our family tend to spend a lot of time in the kitchen. It seems the perfect place to talk.

My parents listened and dad made a remark, which really upset me. He commented the doctors couldn't find anything wrong with me because there was nothing wrong. He didn't say it in a nasty way but it hurt all the same.

I knew I wasn't crazy. I also knew I wasn't a hypochondriac and anyone who knows me will vouch for that. With Malcolm away so much I do everything within my physical capability around the house; gardening, decorating, DIY.

You name it I'll do it. I may not do it as well as a professional but I'll give it a go. It takes my mind off autism apart from saving a fortune, and if a job needs doing I just get on with it.

I'm as tough as old boots normally and have to feel absolutely awful before I'll admit to being ill.

Anyway, It was generally agreed I had mercury toxicity.

My dad said I had it, even if I didn't which on the surface probably doesn't make a lot of sense. What he meant though was as I'd identified with several of the symptoms, I'd made a self-diagnosis, and until it was proven otherwise, I'd convinced myself I had mercury toxicity.

Now do you get it?

Well, he was right and so plans were made to get me tested as soon as possible.

I rang Chris Mascarenhas, explained the situation and how I'd heard of him. Chris agreed to see me, and the following week my parents drove me to his house.

I wasn't a very competent driver at this stage because my eyes kept going funny. It was as though moving patterns would pass across them, which made it difficult to focus.

Also, my left leg kept going numb and I felt I had to keep moving my toes to make sure I could still feel them, which isn’t a great situation to be in when your feet are on the car pedals.

My fingers always had pins and needles in them too but more importantly, I never felt “with it”. Another thing I noticed was that I panicked about silly things like whether I would be able to park.

I’d find myself going shopping as soon as the boys had gone to school just so that I would know that the car park would be almost empty when I arrived.

Whenever I got behind the wheel of the car I had to really concentrate on what I was doing and couldn’t even have the radio on. I was like a learner driver just beginning in a car – very tense. In fact, I’ve been driving for thirty years and am normally considered a careful, woman driver.

I did have one accident though when I wrote our car off.

Jodi had just celebrated his second birthday and Malcolm had left the previous week for what we’d agreed would be a maximum of eighteen months work overseas, but that seems to have been extended somewhat.

At the time we were all lodging with my parents because we were having the house I mentioned earlier built. If you read Jodi’s first book you'll remember we sold it when we attempted to live as a family in Oman.

Unfortunately, he behaved so awfully the attempt only lasted for a few weeks and Malcolm had to stay on in his new job whilst the rest of us returned to the UK.

Anyway, whilst we were staying with my parents, Daryl, Jodi and I slept in one of their bedrooms, or at least Daryl did. Jodi spent most of his time awake, which meant that I was also awake.

I couldn't leave him on his own because he had no sense of danger, and also my dad was a milkman at the time and had to be up early.

Prior to our arrival, dad had been able to sleep in the afternoon but of course that all changed once Jodi appeared on the scene so he certainly needed his "shut eye" as he called it at night.

Invariably, dad would get up at the crack of dawn to find Jodi and me sitting in the dark, watching videos with the sound turned down as low as possible.

As Jodi liked to watch the same videos over and over again, dad would find himself waking his customers up with a whistling rendition of Postman Pat. I suppose it made a change from the birds and the dawn chorus.

One Sunday, on dad's day off, someone suggested going to Banham Zoo so the boys could see all the animals. It wasn't too far away but we had to take two cars as my nephews, who are the same age as Daryl and Jodi, also joined us.

They travelled in the back of dad's car and mum came with me to show the way. We set off in the morning and Jodi had his supply of hoola hoops with him, which was the only thing he would eat at that stage.

It was a nice day, sunny and dry and we spent several hours walking around the zoo, with the three boys looking at the animals and playing on the bouncy castle. Jodi stayed in his buggy not appearing to look at anything, but undoubtedly seeing everything.

We left at about 2 o'clock in the afternoon.

Dad led the way and I followed, but when we got on a road about five miles from home, dad lost sight of me in his rear view mirror. He knew I could make my way home though so he drove all the way back to his house expecting me to turn up a few minutes later.

I didn't, because not long after he'd disappeared from my sight, our car was sideways up in a fifteen-foot ditch, fortunately devoid of water.

Everything happened so fast, but the Mazda 626 is a very strong car and we all had our seat belts on, so instead of it crumpling, it just turned on its side and thankfully we remained in our seats.

Jodi and I were horizontal at the bottom and mum and Daryl were above us. Fortunately it didn't roll over.

The car was a write-off, mum had dreadful bruising caused by the seat belt and her hand has never fully recovered, but Daryl and Jodi were fine. I was pretty shook up by the whole experience and wonder what went wrong. I think I possibly fell asleep at the wheel.

Maybe I had mercury toxicity then or perhaps I was just really tired, I'll never know. I still have nightmares about the episode and what might have happened. Jodi had just come out of hospital having had his first lot of grommets put in.

Unfortunately they hadn't solved his problem despite the £1000 they'd cost us. At the time we had thought Jodi's trouble was pain and deafness caused by glue ear and we'd paid for the operation because the waiting list on the National Health Service (NHS) was far too long.

It was over two more years before we finally realised our son had infact got autism and the grommets wouldn't have helped him anyway.

The thing that haunts me most about the accident though is when we were all safely out of the car and I was hugging the boys, I looked at Jodi, who appeared completely oblivious to what was going on and thought, "Thank goodness we didn't just waste our money".

How awful is that?

Sorry about that detour. I'm trying to slay my demons but back now to my visit with Chris.

The consultation and testing was going to take some time so my parents dropped me off and arranged to collect me later. Chris started by filling in a patient questionnaire form.

He asked several questions and explained he needed to ascertain what my problems were so he could determine just what to test me for. There are literally hundreds of tests that can be performed and it saved time, money and discomfort if these could be narrowed down to the relevant ones.

It was decided I should first be tested for heavy metals and then, if he felt it appropriate, Chris would recommend I have my hormones tested as well. This was optional but could be beneficial to my health. It would, however, cost more.

You have to realise currently there's nothing available like this on the NHS and such testing isn't widely recognised. The argument from the Health Authorities and the Private Health companies is there's no regulation within the alternative medicine industry and anyone can set up as a practitioner.

They say the tests are only as good as the people who translate them. You see there are a lot of charlatans around who make a lot of money out of sick and vulnerable people.

Apparently it's possible to manipulate test results especially if you have some idea what the client is expecting to find, so be warned.

After the grommet incident with Jodi we took out private medical insurance, but I wasn't able to make a claim for the testing or subsequent supplements used because they said this type of treatment "has not been established as being effective".

You would have thought the NHS and the medical insurance companies would be interested in anything that could make people well, but then, maybe not.

By virtue of the professions they're in, doctors and medical health insurers need people to either be ill, or anticipate they might be, or they'd be out of a job.

Preventative medicine isn't always highly thought of.

It's bizarre.

Anyway, Chris tests by a method called EDS (Electro-dermal screening), which is a totally non-invasive, painless, computerised screening process, used on people of any age or condition.

It can be used as I may already have mentioned to accurately screen the body for food sensitivities, levels of vitamins and minerals, amino acids, fatty acids, blood sugars and enzymes, hormonal levels and other health indicators.

It helps assess exactly what treatment is needed as it also identifies nutritional imbalances in the body.

There are other types of tests you can have to find out similar information. The most accepted tests by the medical profession are the blood ones.

It's possible to get Live Blood Analysis done whereby a sample of your blood can be taken from your finger, placed on slides and looked at through a microscope connected to a screen.

You can see instantly what's happening inside you and why. I didn't have that done initially, but have had one since. It's really interesting.

Another simple test, is by using saliva and litmus paper. It's quick, simple and cheap and can determine whether a person has heavy metal toxicity, but doesn't go into detail like the other tests.

The test I had consisted of holding a metal rod in my left hand, which acted as a conductor between the computer and me.

Chris then touched an acupressure point on the middle finger of my right hand with a special metal probe, which produced an immediate graph reading on the computer screen.

It was accompanied by an audible noise, which indicated whether my body was weakened, balanced or stressed for the particular item being tested for.

It was great because I could immediately see I had the following: arsenic 62, lead 61, aluminium 61, nickel 58, cadmium metallicum 56, and mercury 63.

Chris explained why each thing was so important and what role it played in my health. At the time though my brain was about as clear as mud so I can't remember half of what he told me.

I do know the normal baseline of readings is 50 though, so anything above or below that is either stressed or weakened.

I was tested for 116 things and only 16 were balanced.

My fears about mercury were realised but I was surprised about the others.

I guessed the lead could have come from petrol fumes and paint. I'm always painting. It's a joke in our house that if anything keeps still for more than two minutes, I'll paint it.

However, the arsenic was a bit of a mystery. If Malcolm had been home more I might have accused him of attempting to poison me, but of course that was ridiculous.

Chris explained it used to be in rodent controls and certain paints. We'd purchased a plot of land next to the house where we now live a few years ago, and this used to be a builders yard.

It was dreadfully overgrown and had been unused for twenty years. It was full of everything you could think of including old cars; asbestos sheds, building materials, railway sleepers, and rats.

I cleared a lot of it myself and initially had to hack my way through the blackberry bushes and stinging nettles, which were head high with a machete. I also helped empty the sheds and put most of the contents into a skip after I'd rummaged around to see what was there.

It's likely, I got some rat poison on me, as often I didn't wear gloves and when I did they tended to get ripped by the various things I handled.

Also, arsenic used to be used in some older vaginal pessaries and I'd suffered from thrush several years earlier so I may have got it from that. It's in all sorts of everyday items though and once you're in the position of not being able to get rid of it, even the most miniscule amount can become a potential hazard.

Anyway, how I got it was irrelevant, I was more interested in how I could get rid of it.

I had the heavy metal, hormone and nutritional tests and Chris told me not to worry and that I'd be okay.

Easy for him to say – he wasn't the one with all the toxins in his body. He told me I needed to look after myself more as I had obviously been concentrating too much on everyone else.

I felt too dazed to argue. All that information and all the stressed and weakened figures had made me feel quite ill.

He recommended an anti-oxidation (de-tox) and a nutritional protocol for me to follow. He told me to get my amalgam fillings removed SAFELY half way through the de-tox. For the de-tox programme, he recommended I use Humet®-R to remove all the heavy metals.

When my parents returned to collect me I'd had time to come to terms with the results and felt relieved and vindicated. At last I'd found someone who'd confirmed I did indeed have something wrong with me and I wasn't going mad.

I asked Chris if he'd relay this information to my dad, which he did, and if he ever reads this story dad will realise how much his earlier comment hurt me, even though I knew he hadn't done so intentionally.

Many people with heavy metal toxicity get deeply upset because people disbelieve the way they feel. It seems if symptoms don't fit snugly inside a medical label, they can't exist, and many people exhaust themselves pretending to be fine when in reality they feel awful.

I obtained all the tablets and capsules Chris recommended as soon as possible, but I couldn't start my de-tox until I'd arranged to have my amalgam fillings removed.

I went to visit my dentist in Littleport for a quick chat. Michael Young is incredibly busy as he is a NHS dentist who also does private work. He works long hours but does have Friday afternoons off when the surgery is closed.

I explained the position to him and showed him the test results. It was clear I was anxious to get the amalgam out of my mouth by the tremble in my voice and the tears in my eyes. I felt really out of control and frightened.

Mr. Young looked in my mouth and at his records to see just how many teeth required re-filling. There were seven. I had huge amalgam fillings where there were more grey amalgam than teeth and felt like Jaws out of that James Bond movie.

I've often been asked why I look so serious in photographs but my teeth have never been my best assets so I don't flash them unless I have to.

Michael explained it was going to be a long and expensive job. You see whilst you can get amalgam fillings put in on the NHS you can't get them removed under the same system.

My medical health insurance didn't cover teeth either, and although I argued I was having the treatment for health reasons rather than cosmetic, they declined to pay.

I discussed the process with Michael and asked if he could remove the fillings. Of course I knew he could remove the fillings but I wanted to be absolutely certain he could do it safely.

I'd read many people have been incredibly ill after they'd had amalgam fillings removed because the procedure hadn't been carried out with the utmost care.

You see once you start messing around with the fillings there's an increased likelihood for even more mercury vapour to be released. If you aren't de-toxing properly it could settle in your organs and tissue and make you worse than you were before.

Also, unless a rubber dam is used there is a great possibility of you swallowing parts of the filling as it's drilled out.

Michael assured me whilst he wasn't a mercury-free dentist, he could carry out my wishes, and it was agreed the best way forward would be for me to have the whole seven fillings removed in one go.

He said he'd replace them with temporary fillings and then I could have composite fillings fitted as and when it was convenient.

Many sources say you shouldn't take that route, but should have the fillings removed slowly over a period of time. It's also recommended by some, the procedure be done in quadrants, with those teeth having the highest negative charge removed first.

I just wanted to get the metal out of my mouth as quickly as possible though as I was feeling worse by the day. I reasoned that if I was following a de-toxification programme I'd be okay and I was.

At this point I should also point out the possible dangers of some root canal work as I'm informed this can cause all sorts of long-term adverse reactions. I'm not sure if I had the type of throbbing pain usually associated with the urgent need to have it done I'd take that into consideration though.

A root canal is when the nerve is removed from the tooth and the root tip is filled and sealed. It can be done in two ways; conventionally which is through the tooth, or surgically in an operation called an apicectomy.

In the past amalgam was used in the surgical type to seal the root apex, but I'm told non-metallic materials such as composite are used these days. I'm also told the conventional way is not considered dangerous.

What I'm saying here is if you have your fillings removed don't forget to check on any root canal work you may have had done just incase amalgam was used.

Also you need to be aware of crowns, as I've been told many dentists use amalgam to restore the crown of the tooth.

If you're concerned about your health and your doctors can't come up with a reason for your symptoms perhaps you should consider any dental work you've had done including caps, crowns, bridges or braces.

I recommend you read. Dr. Hal A Huggins book "It's All In Your Head". It's very enlightening especially the relationship between the different electrical currents created by the various metals. The battery like activity in your mouth can be quite traumatic apparently.

But back to the story, and my dentist kindly offered to work one Friday afternoon so he could take all my fillings out.

He arranged for his dental nurse to work also and I felt terrible about that because it was the school holidays and the weather was amazing. It was dry, sunny and very warm, not the kind of afternoon you want to be stuck in a dental surgery.

Anyway I turned up at one o'clock and arranged to telephone Malcolm when I'd finished, which I anticipated would be at about four. I'd been told it would take roughly three hours, which is a long time to sit with your mouth open and not be able to talk.

Actually, come to think of it, three minutes is a long time for me not to talk when I'm in company, unless I'm listening of course.

I spend so much time with children who either can't or won't talk, I'm always glad of a bit of conversation whenever possible.

I find though on the rare occasions when Malcolm's home I tend to let him do most of the talking if we're in company. I always feel he and his life are far more interesting than mine and that appears to be the case for most mothers I know of autistic children.

We all appear to be under the illusion the only thing we can talk about with confidence is our offspring. That's understandable though as autism does have a way of taking over and affecting far more than just the person with the disability.

Anyway, Michael fitted a rubber dam over each tooth in turn as he worked, using a high-powered drill to remove the fillings as quickly as possible. The rubber dam is a piece of square or rectangular rubber, with a single hole in it.

You place the hole over the tooth to be worked on and secure it with a clamp. The rubber is then stretched over the whole of your mouth and secured on a sort of framework. This means that the dentist can only see the tooth he's working on.

He then tests to ensure there are no leaks by letting some water run on the top of the rubber and making certain it doesn't run through into the patient's mouth. If everything's okay it's safe to begin.

I was happy to lie in the chair; relieved I was doing something constructive to get my health back. I didn't even mind too much not being able to talk, although I would have loved to have had a bit of a conversation with the dental nurse as I caught her looking longingly out of the window and felt really sorry for her.

About half way through the session though, I had to signal for the dentist to stop. You see on the ceiling of the surgery, directly above the patient's chair was a painting done by one of Michael's friends.

It's a lovely scene with a rowing boat tethered by a huge lake and mountains in the background. Looking at it became a form of torture for me though because on the de-tox I had to drink at least 3 litres of filtered water each day.

Water is really good for you anyway but on a de-tox you need more to flush all the toxins through the body.

Consequently I had to empty my bladder frequently and lying there, looking at that lake, was making me very uncomfortable. Even closing my eyes didn't help so when Michael was about to work on a different tooth I asked to be excused.

I think he was a bit worried I wasn't feeling too well until I explained and then he laughed.

It took about three and a half hours to get all the amalgam out of my mouth and have strong temporary fillings put back in.

I made three more, one and a half hour appointments, to have the composite ones put in and now that they're all done I don't mind smiling again. I no longer feel like Jaws, but more importantly, I'm no longer being poisoned.

One interesting fact I discovered, which perhaps you don't know, is your teeth are connected to various parts of your body. The type of reactions you can have and the areas affected will depend on the tooth or teeth having treatment.

Incredible isn't it?

Imagine having a bad toe because you've had a tooth filled sometime previously. Now that really would be Foot and Mouth!

Another thing I should point out here though, and this is VERY important, is if you are mercury toxic, just having your amalgam fillings out won't cure you.

It will prevent any more leaking from your teeth into your body, but you'll still have the same amount of mercury inside you. This will still be attached to your fat binding organs and will continue to cause problems, so you have to get it out of your system.

The way to do it is by means of using some form of chelation.

The one Bryan, I, and many others have used successfully is called Humet®-R. At the end of the book I've written about this incredible product in more detail, but for now all you need to know is it's sold as a health supplement and comes from a natural source.

Actually it comes from a peat bog which runs along the north shore of Lake Balaton in Hungary, and you can't get much more natural than that. In terms of peat bogs it's quite new apparently, somewhere between 3 and 10,000 years old!

Another person who knows all about the benefits of Humet®-R and is deserving of a mention is Pam Clayton.

Her health had deteriorated for 20 years. It started with asthma, then IBS, dizzy spells, headaches, numbness and tingling throughout her body and pains in her arms and legs.

As if that wasn't enough, her memory drastically deteriorated, she always felt as if she had a hangover, had difficulty swallowing, couldn't stand noise and didn't want to socialise. Her legs kept giving way and sometimes she just couldn't get out of bed.

The doctors couldn't find anything wrong with her, and finally when she reached the point where she could hardly breathe to talk to people, she visited a practitioner with a written list of all her symptoms.

He diagnosed mercury toxicity from her amalgam fillings and advised she get them removed. Pam found a mercury-free dentist and began her long road to recovery.

That was in 1997 and now she's much better but it's been a hard process. Her symptoms kept coming back over a period of three years because her immune system was so weak, and as they did so, she went on the de-tox again.

She'll never be completely cured and has had to give up work because when something affects her she has to take time off. However, she is now able to live life fully again and is making up for lost time.

As a result of her illness, Pam set up a helpline for people who had been suffering from various symptoms caused by mercury leaking from their dental amalgams. She has over 6,000 people on it and I'm one of them.

If you want to check it out just go to www.pamshelpline.co.uk., or you can e-mail her at: pam@mercury-helpline.freeserve.co.uk. It's quite an eye opener.

Pam is a very busy person now, answering e-mails, letters and telephone calls relating to mercury toxicity. She's also written her own book which you can find information on by contacting her website.

Another thing she's doing is spending long overdue time with her grandchildren whom she's only just come to know because of her earlier health problems.

Pam is an incredible lady and her husband must also be wonderful to share her with so many needy people.

Jodi - 2

Right, that's it. I've let mum ramble on for long enough and it's about time I got hold of the reins again. This is, after all, a continuation of "my" story – right?

Okay then, mum had her teeth sorted, finished her de-tox and went back to see Chris. She felt much better by the time of her appointment and many of her worrying symptoms had already disappeared.

She actually felt in control of her life but still didn't drive over there. This time dad was home, and as it was during the school holidays, we all went along.

Mum had decided we all ought to be tested. This mercury thing had really got her worried. Anyway, she went first and was really pleased to discover that her heavy metal levels had dropped considerably and she no longer had any that were stressed.

Mercury had dropped from 63 to 33, arsenic from 62 to 21, lead from 61 to 27, aluminium from 61 to 37, nickel from 58 to 20, and cadmium metallicum from 56 to 20. She knew she felt better and now she knew why.

I was the next to be tested but I didn't particularly like the acupressure point on my finger being prodded with the metal probe. It was okay for a couple of goes but then it got a bit sensitive and I didn't want to play so mum was used as my surrogate.

The way that worked was I held the metal rod in my hand to act as the conductor and then mum held her hand over mine to make sure I kept the connection. Chris then used her finger to check my readings.

I have to admit I felt a bit sorry for her as she'd already had her test done with numerous prods and then had to have the same acupressure point used again for mine. (I didn't feel sufficiently sorry to use my finger instead though).

Well, the results were as mum expected, at least as far as mercury was concerned because my level was even higher than hers had been originally – 64. I was also stressed for lead, 63, aluminium, 63, and actinium, 60.

What the test also revealed was that all my nutritional vitamins, minerals, sugars, amino acids and fatty acids were dramatically weakened, as were many of my hormones.

I also had high levels of bacteria, parasites and fungi. My candida level was 60, which seems to be a problem for many autists.

Candida, if you didn't know refers to a condition in which an overgrowth of yeast in the body can overwhelm the immune system.

It's normally kept in check by 'good' bacteria living in our guts, where it competes with oxygen to survive. However, subtle hormonal changes can cause the yeast to change its form so it no longer needs oxygen to survive and it puts down roots in the walls of the intestine and burrows into the rest of the body.

That's what causes leaky gut syndrome and allows toxins, which would normally be passed through the gut to enter the bloodstream.

There's a theory the widespread use of antibiotics is one of the reasons for the increase of candida because they kill off not only the bad bacteria but also the good ones.

I had lots of antibiotics when I was small as I had lots of ear infections so the theory makes sense, at least to me.

Candida can be treated though and in my case I used a product called Citricidal, which is a grapefruit seed extract and comes in either liquid or capsule form.

Chris worked out a de-tox and nutritional programme specifically for my needs at the time and wished mum good luck in getting me to follow it. You'll find out why soon.

Next up was my dad who actually felt incredibly healthy, but he had heavy metal toxicity too. Finally, Daryl was tested. He'd been suffering from a bad stomach for years and frequently had to dash off to the toilet as soon as he'd eaten something.

The result could be quite explosive but thankfully mum has taught him how to use the toilet brush and cleaner. The windows got opened quite often too.

Also, if you remember, he'd complained of not being able to see clearly sometimes, and his memory was getting dreadful.

Mum was partly reassured by other parents of teenagers telling her their offspring were just the same, but there were occasions when dad would ask her jokingly, "Are you sure he's mine?" He just couldn't believe some of the things Daryl would do, or forget to do.

Once again mercury came up trumps. His level was the same as mine, 64. He also had molybdenum, 60, lead, 57, aluminium, 57 and actinium, 55.

Daryl was also given a de-tox and nutritional programme to follow. We left some three hours later, arms full of supplements, bank devoid of funds.

Dad suddenly felt ill.

Daryl and dad started their programmes straight away but mum was afraid to start my de-tox fully because I needed to be able to take all the tablets and capsules, and to drink enough filtered water to flush all the toxins through my system.

I rarely ever drank water – at least not plain water. I would have it flavoured with fruit juice, which was okay as a last resort, but ideally plain old filtered water was best

It needed to be filtered as opposed to tap, bottled or fizzy water because of the nitrates.

Another thing I needed to do was take all the supplements. You see I will chew tablets but I won't entertain capsules and some of the supplements were in capsule form including the Humet®-R.

There were quite a few and I had to take them three times a day, at least for the first month.

Initially, I started taking everything but the Humet®-R and it took me nearly all day to get them down. It didn't matter too much because it was the school holidays but it was pretty stressful and a waste of time.

You see I would insist every tablet was cut into four pieces. I would put each quarter in my mouth and chew it before washing it down with a drink.

I emptied every capsule into a medicine spoon and then put the dry contents into my mouth before once again washing them down with more drink.

This wasn't a quick process though because I had to build up to it. I would walk around the house with a medicine spoon full of powder held out in front of me as though I was entering an egg and spoon race, talking to myself and recounting familiar stories that comforted me, and then, when I felt ready, I'd pause and swallow the powder.

By the time I'd finished each session of tablets at least two hours had passed and I'd drunk my two litres of water. I spent the next few hours peeing in the toilet before starting the whole thing all over again.

You see the tablets are to be taken with food. Well some are taken half an hour before food, some with, and the others after. My protocol sort of merged all together but I wouldn't be hurried.

On the day my dad was due to go back to his job overseas, he kept telling me to, "hurry up" and followed me around on my travels with my medicine spoons.

I got a bit stressed, which is a slight understatement. Actually I went ballistic and hit him really hard. I've never done that to him before and we were both surprised.

I cried and screamed as I lashed out, but he just held my wrists really tight and forced me down onto the settee, so I kicked him – hard.

My brother, by this time, was declaring it was the tablets, that they were doing more harm than good and that I should stop taking them.

Mum told him he didn't know what he was talking about and to keep out of it.

He was clearly upset and rushed outside, so mum became referee in the one-sided fight still going on in the lounge.

She called time, sent dad outside to check that Daryl was all right, and told me, "It's okay". She held me close, wiped away the tears and told me I mustn't smack.

I kept repeating, "It's okay", "It's okay" through my sobs and eventually I calmed down.

It was the first and last time I got upset about taking my tablets and when dad came in from the garden, I instinctively rubbed his arm and legs and said "that's better".

Mum told me also to say "sorry". I obliged but no one really knew if I understood the meaning of the word.

Daryl was distressed and it was clear he'd been crying. Mum comforted him and he even allowed her to cuddle him and kiss the top of his head, which is not a "cool" thing for a teenager to have his mum do, so my outburst must really have upset him.

She explained I had to continue with my tablets even though it was difficult because it could help me considerably. She said it wasn't surprising I'd been upset as I was being hassled to take all these tablets and capsules and didn't understand why.

Also, unlike him, who could swallow them whole, I was chewing them and eating the dry powder, which must have tasted awful.

He understood eventually but said he was really upset because he was afraid I'd turn on her. If I hit mum with the force with which I hit and kicked my dad, she'd be very badly injured.

It's common knowledge autists are amazingly strong and I'm no exception. Daryl also said if I hit him, he'd hit me back, but even though he's bigger and older than me, I think I'm stronger.

At the back of it all though, I think Daryl was really upset because dad was going away yet again.

Now apart from the candida already mentioned, another thing common to many autists is intolerance towards gluten and casein. These are the proteins found in wheat, oats, barley and rye, and in dairy products.

There are many books written on the subject, and the tests Chris did revealed my brother, who is not autistic, was suffering from them too. His stress test reading for gluten was 72 and that's pretty stressed. It accounted for his rapid visits to the toilet after eating.

We'd both had our urine tested a few years earlier and I'd discovered then I had the problem, but at the time Daryl was okay. Consequently my diet had changed somewhat but his remained the same.

I have a self-restricted diet anyway but the few things I did eat containing wheat disappeared from my plate and mostly I have gluten free pasta, etc.

My meals, as I mentioned earlier, are dry and hard which is one obvious reason why my mum was unable to disguise the contents of the capsules for my nutrition and de-toxification protocol in any of my food. I would have noticed immediately and refused to eat.

Another reason she didn't attempt it though, was because if the powders were added to heated foods, then the natural bioactive enzymes could be destroyed so I was stuck with my spoonfuls of powder.

I stopped having normal cows milk years ago when my diet changed and went on to soya, but Chris advised this probably wasn't a good choice for me because of my autism. He recommended either rice or sheep milk because soya concentrates aluminium during its growth phase.

His explanation was aluminium is a neuro toxin, which means it affects the nervous system, and is associated with major central brain illness conditions.

Autists are particularly at risk from high aluminium levels because part of their condition stems from brain disruption caused by toxicity and low levels of key nutrients, so basically they need to steer clear of it where possible.

Goat milk is similar to soya but contains less fat and has the advantage of being beneficial to patients who are sensitive to albumin, casein and lactose.

Sheep milk was okay but we couldn't find any initially so rice milk got the thumbs up and we used that for a while. It's an acquired taste though and once mum managed to locate a supplier of dried sheep milk we changed. She still buys small cartons of semi-skimmed milk for any visitors though.

Apparently mercury interferes with digestive enzymes and many people who are mercury toxic have food sensitivities. It also causes damage to the immune system, which allows yeast and bacteria to build up.

This yeast overgrowth can cause the "leaky gut" condition I mentioned earlier, where the lining of the intestine becomes porous and allows undigested food particles to enter the bloodstream, resulting in allergic reactions.

It's a bit like having a colander inside you and theoretically, once the mercury is removed, the immune system is restored, the gut heals and regular foods can be re-introduced because the holes in the colander get filled in.

Now doesn't that sound much better than being on a gluten and casein free diet all your life – considerably cheaper too?

Daryl hoped it would work because although he became quite used to his gluten free diet and said the rice milk was "okay actually", he still looked longingly at the cream cakes, pizzas, chocolate, etc.

Chris said it would take at least a couple of months to sort him out and Daryl should have known by November whether his holes had been plugged, but mum decided to drag it out a bit longer just to make sure. I hope Daryl doesn't read this, as I don't think he knows about that.

I can report his memory got much better, he never complains of headaches or his eyes going funny any more and I no longer get flattened in his rush to get to the toilet after a meal.

Mum also gets conversations out of him. Now that really is progress!

Dad, on the other hand, says he felt worse after taking the tablets but that's maybe because he was still recovering from the shock of the cost of everything. No actually everyone who knows anything about de-toxing has said he probably didn't drink enough water.

You see dad started his de-tox about a week before he left. He works on a little island just off Iran at the moment and says the water there is "unfit for human consumption" because it's so salty.

Almost everything is done with bottled water, including washing down the helicopter engines on which he works and one of the people he works with even heats bottled water to shower in.

It also gets incredibly hot over there and when he was on his de-tox it was about forty degrees plus. People sweat a lot, or perspire if you like, so most of the recommended two litres of bottled water dad drank each day most likely came out of his pores rather than flushing through his system and into the toilet.

Don't misunderstand here, dad doesn't feel ill, just no better than he did before, whereas mum and Daryl feel great.

One real improvement mum has had is that she can sleep now. Prior to her treatment, she suffered from insomnia and was always up in the middle of the night reading, ironing, or on the computer or something.

I used to hear her downstairs and would lay awake reciting Thomas stories until she came back to bed and settled down again. I was sort of watching over her I guess – talk about role reversal!

Mum said she felt tired, but just couldn't sleep. Apparently the mercury had played havoc with her hormones and her melatonin, the hormone that tells your brain to switch off, was really low.

She could only sleep at night if she was physically exhausted. Now she stays in bed all night long.

Dad's pleased!

Okay, you might say, that's all very well but as this story is about me, how do I feel?

For a start I'm considerably calmer and very willing to join in all the activities at school. I started a new class in September with a different teacher and only some of the pupils I'd been with previously.

I wasn't fazed by all the changes though and I settled in straight away. I've received several class certificates and Head Teacher's Awards for good work already.

My mum has this really good system going with the school by means of a Home to School diary. She writes in it things she feels the teacher should know about what I've done at home and the teacher tells her how I've spent my school day.

It means mum or my teacher can attempt to get an appropriate conversation out of me. I have one for my Respite Care home too and that way all three areas know what's going on in my life.

As I keep saying, my vocabulary is limited and I usually only speak if I have to, so would be unable to relay the sort of information these diaries contain.

Apart from repeating whole chunks of videos, I generally only use single nouns and then only really for things I want or need, but I have improved – a lot.

On the day before I started back to school mum started my full de-tox. She had, by this time, managed to get me to take all the tablets and capsules in a reasonable time, using a strategy of locking the door to my special room with the two-way mirror and hiding the key.

I wasn't allowed in there until I had taken my "before" tablets.

Once they were down I could watch a video or go on the computer or something for a few minutes until my meal was ready. I then had to come out, the door was relocked and I wasn't allowed back in until I had eaten my meal and taken my "with" and "after" tablets.

Obviously if I wanted to go back into the room, I needed to "hurry up". I hate being told that normally but when needs must…

Mum no longer locks the room because I know what's expected of me. I just take the tablets and the time taken to get them down now depends on what I want to do afterwards.

In fact, I get the tablets and cut them up myself if mum forgets to do it. I can use the pill cutter and I know just what I have to take and when.

I no longer walk around the house with my medicine spoons, but just line everything up on the kitchen table and take them in the same order each time.

Also, I no longer take Humet®-R every day but I know mum is considering giving me another dose soon to see if I make any more improvements.

It's no big deal any more as I only have to take one of the capsules, thirty minutes after my main meal. Out of its shell the mixture looks like a medicine spoon full of gunpowder but I can handle it.

Initially mum used to get me up at six o'clock so I'd be ready to catch the taxi at twenty-five past eight in the morning, but that no longer applies. Seven o'clock is just fine.

It gives me time to have a shower, get dressed, take my tablets, have my breakfast, go to the toilet, clean my teeth and get my bag and coat ready.

Sometimes I even watch the video for a few minutes. The taxi drivers are really nice though and wouldn't mind waiting for me if necessary, although to date that has never been the case.

I even carry my coat and bag to the taxi myself now, which is something I never used to do - I'd make mum carry it.

What's that expression my dad jokingly uses, "you don't have a dog and bark"?

I no longer insist on sitting in the same place and take whichever seat is vacant on the taxi. I put my seat belt on and wave and say "goodbye" to my mum.

Previously I would look the other way or straight ahead. Mind you there's a railway line a few metres along the road from our house and I love to watch the trains go over the crossing so that may have something to do with it.

Anyway, I want to tell you about a trip to the library taken not long after I started my de-tox. In our class we walk up to the library in Ely about once every two to three weeks and we are all allowed to choose two books, which we take back to school.

They are kept in class and we read them.

On the first trip to the library I chose two "Spot" books. Actually I chose a lot more but was only allowed to take two back with me. Caroline, my teacher wrote this information in my Home to School diary.

That night when mum was giving me a bath she asked me what I'd done at school.

Normally, I just repeat "school" in echolalia fashion and look at her blankly, but this particular evening we had a bit of a conversation. It went something like this:

"What did you do at school today, Jodi?"

"School"

"Did you go for a walk?"

"Walk"

"Where did you go?"

"Go"

"Did you go to the library?"

"Library"

"What did you get?"

"Books" – (Progress!)

"How many did you get?"

"Two"

"What were they about?"

"Spot"

"What were they called?"

"Spot's Windy Day, Spot Follows His Nose"

"That's great Jodi, Well done"

Mum was really impressed but then I confused her a bit by mentioning two more Spot book titles so she wasn't completely sure that I had understood what she was talking about.

However, she was incredibly chuffed because for the first time ever she'd held a conversation with me where my replies hadn't been prompted by visual clues, or where the subject of the session had just happened.

She wrote about it in the book to Caroline who suggested maybe the other two titles I'd mentioned had been those of the books I'd been made to return to the shelves in the library.

It sounded feasible but then two days later mum received another note in the diary to say when they'd checked my books they discovered there was more than one story in each of them and the other titles I'd mentioned, "Spot Visits His Grandparents", and "Spot In The Snow", were in fact included in them too.

What do you think about that – deserving of a Head Teacher's Award or what?

Caroline, my teacher has said of me, and here I quote, "Jodi is a real pleasure to have in the class in many ways. He is always co-operative, helpful and it is so lovely to have someone so tidy! I am enjoying teaching him".

Isn't that nice?

Not long into the school term, for the first time ever, I was included in the whole class numeracy "starter" session.

We'd been developing counting skills, pretty basic stuff like counting in 1s, 2s and 10s. In the session each pupil had to use a mini whiteboard and write the number, which would follow a short sequence written on the board, e.g. 97, 98, 99 ----, 2, 4 ,6, ----, 60, 70 ,80 ----.

You get the idea?

No one was allowed to speak and we pupils had to hold up our boards to show the answers. I got all mine right except one and Caroline was really pleased with my understanding of what needed to be done and my grasp of sequences.

I faltered on 35 ,45 ,55 ---. I wrote 66 but then so did several other pupils so I don't think that was bad. Mum didn't either.

I also impressed her with the way I described a video I was watching the other day. It was Fantasia 2000 but I have only mastered counting up to 100 so far.

When she asked me what film it was, I replied, "Fantasia twenty-zero-zero". Pretty clever, don't you think?

I spend more time with my brother now too and help him change the water in our fish tanks. We used to have three and our house looked a bit like an aquarium so we've now reduced it to two.

Fish are so relaxing though. They're quiet, don't invade my space and can't creep up on me unexpectedly. I like them.

We also play a bit of golf and tennis together, "bit" being the operative word, but it's something that never happened before. I copy him a lot when we're together which is supposed to be a compliment.

If he takes his jumper off, mine comes off too, he puts his sunglasses on, out come mine, that sort of thing. (He's dreading bringing a girlfriend home). It does come in handy though if my parents want me to learn something.

We went to Skegness one day and decided to play bowls. It's a game only dad had played before but you can hire the woods, the mats and the jack for an hour for a reasonable price so we decided to give it a go.

The man in the kiosk explained the rules of the game and we took our rink.

My mum noticed that sitting on a bench watching us were two women and a smartly dressed man in a black blazer adorned with lots of badges.

She guessed he might be an expert, so when we changed ends she greeted him with a cheery, "We haven't got a clue what we're doing", and he came over.

He must have been in his seventies and had, he told us, been bowling since he was eleven. He'd played for England and was now a coach at Boston – in England that is.

The man told us all about the bias and how to determine which way the wood would go.

He demonstrated how to stand and bowl the woods by manipulating Daryl as he took his position. My turn was next and I soon walked up to the spot and allowed the man to do exactly the same to me.

I never usually let any stranger close to me and certainly don't let them manhandle me so this was quite an event. I actually won that "end" and for every throw afterwards I assumed the correct position.

Julian, my homeopath, is amazed at how calm I've become when I visit him. I sit quiet and still in a chair for a whole twenty minutes just listening to mum and him talk instead of getting up and down like a yo-yo, chattering away, banging things and looking out of the window.

I label my own envelopes and put my pills into them so all Julian has to do is sprinkle the correct homeopathic remedy on.

Currently he's treating me for some tiny spots on my chest and upper arms, which is an age thing to do with a rush of histamine.

The doctor gave me some aqueous cream to put on as soap seems to bring them out more, but Julian has given me some homeopathic remedy to help me get through the hormonal stage.

I cried in class one day for seemingly no apparent reason and everyone was worried about me. I couldn't tell them what was wrong, obviously, and maybe there wasn't anything.

My mum's friend's daughter and my cousin have both been known to do the same thing and they are both the same age as me, so we're guessing it's the hormones!

At my respite care home I'm now with the older children and we learn independence skills. We also go out sometimes to the cinema, restaurants, shopping etc., and have £5 pocket money to spend.

I don't understand money so have to rely on the adults to look after that for me but I do know that you have to pay for things now and will queue up when I've chosen something to buy instead of just walking out the shop.

Mum had a bit of an awkward moment with me recently when we were queuing. We stood behind three adults who clearly had disabilities in one form or another.

It was a Saturday morning and I suspect they were out spending their money for a weekend treat as they were buying magazines, drinks, sweets, etc.

Anyway, the chap infront of mum couldn't speak but held up a wrestling magazine to show her. He had a big grin on his face and was clearly very pleased with his purchase.

Mum smiled at him and asked, by means of pointing, whether the big muscled specimen on the cover was him. The man nodded his head vigorously and laughed.

He then decided to get a 2 litre bottle of Coke, a bar of chocolate and a box of Maltesers. This time though he showed his purchases to me.

Of course, I thought he was giving them to me so I went to take them from him. This upset him very much obviously, and I got upset because I couldn't understand why he would snatch them back when he'd only just offered them to me.

I kept saying my usual "No smacking, no smacking" which makes mum cringe. It's my way of saying "No" or that I don't want something to happen but people must think mum hits me and she never has.

It was a strange situation for a while but mum saved the day by placating me with a small bottle of Coke and a packet of Maltesers.

I must be getting better, No - make that worse, not long ago I would have held out for the 2 litre Coke and the box of Maltesers!

At respite we're encouraged to join in as much as possible and I help in the kitchen. I set and clear the table, cook my own dinner (pasta) and cut up carrots (not for me silly, they're vegetables) – all under close supervision of course. Perhaps I'll be a chef.

On a recent visit whilst I was in the kitchen washing up, I had my back to the care worker and was chattering away to myself. My carer couldn't understand a word I was saying, so she said, "If you want to talk to me you'll have to turn round".

I did, straight away and said, "towel please" as clear as anything.

Now this was really amazing because I'd realised she was talking to me when I wasn't even facing her, she didn't use my name, and also I clearly understood exactly what she said and responded appropriately. Yet another brownie point, I think.

On that same visit I also walked to the post box with the same person. She pointed out a cat to me because she knows I am still frightened of them and didn't want it to take me by surprise incase I jumped into the road in front of a car.

She said it was a "beautiful cat" and I corrected her by saying it was a "beautiful brown cat".

I told a man working on a roof to, "be careful man", I counted all the letters as I posted them into the box and said the colours of all the cars as they passed by.

Paula was very impressed because I'd volunteered the language and used it appropriately. She couldn't wait to tell mum all about it when she came to pick me up after my "one sleep".

I've also begun to read books much to mum's delight but I know she's sometimes a bit confused as to what I actually read and what I remember.

Until very recently I only turned the pages very fast and skimmed the words unless forced to slow down. I didn't attempt to read aloud at all.

I got some books for Christmas though and mum encourages me to read something to her every day.

One of the books was a Thomas the Tank Engine one (no surprise there) and I've seen the episodes in the book hundreds of time on video so can recite the stories off by heart.

However, when my mum asks me to read from that book, I read a few words, or even a complete sentence, using my finger (or hers) to follow each word. I always stop at the end of a sentence, or paragraph and pick up again at the appropriate place.

I like my mum to repeat what I've said after me and then read it aloud herself. I've heard her tell other people she thinks it's my way of reinforcing the words and confirming I've pronounced them correctly as I still don't speak very clearly.

She's asked other people to listen to me read and let her know whether they think I'm actually reading or just remembering.

They all say I'm reading because of the way I move my finger along and really concentrate on the words, knowing exactly what they are and where they fit in the story.

Also if I don't know a word I'll stop and look at the person listening to me and prompt them to tell me what it is.

I do make an attempt to read words by sounding the first one or two letters. Recently it was National Book Day and our class walked in to town to buy a book each.

I chose Duck's Day Out and mum was delighted to learn from my teacher that I'd read it to her as soon as we'd got back to school.

At this rate I'll be on to Harry Potter and Lord of the Rings next, but as it appears my reading abilities are achieved more from memory than from the usual manner in which children learn I doubt I'd ever finish them.

Mum is convinced getting the heavy metals from my body can only help me improve, and the results so far, as I've said, are very positive.

One thing you're bound to be asking though is how did I get them inside me in the first place? Am I right?

Well, it all comes back to mum's teeth and a bit more besides, but because I don't understand it all, I'm going to hand you back to "Sherlock Shaw"

Jean - 2

Now Jodi has introduced me again, I'll pass on what I've discovered about mercury poisoning and the possible link to autism. You can form your own opinion.

As you know mercury vapour gets into the bloodstream and when a woman is pregnant, the developing foetus is fed by blood via her placenta. Horrible though it may seem, it's therefore actually possible for the baby to be poisoned in the womb.

Some people even say it can happen before then, because if the father has mercury in his bloodstream the child could be affected upon conception.

There's a thought.

Okay then, here's how I think it happened in Jodi's case.

Malcolm may or may not have had any mercury in his bloodstream when Jodi was conceived but I most certainly had lots in mine during the early stage of his pregnancy.

I had three enormous amalgam fillings done and not because it was free. We were over in Brunei at the time and part of Malcolm's contract was that we would receive free dental and medical treatment.

I pass that bit of information on so you won't think I just had the fillings done because I was pregnant.

You see in UK, until a few years ago, pregnant women and those who'd recently given birth were given free dental treatment and there are many women who'll admit they saved up their dental work for that specific reason.

I've read the first three months of pregnancy is when the baby is most susceptible and since mercury from the mother's fillings can cross the placental barrier, damage can be done in seconds.

At the time I had my fillings I remember thinking how lucky I was the dentist was willing to undertake the work.

The fillings I required were huge and I ended up with far more amalgam than tooth in all of them.

I'd quite thought he'd tell me he'd have to remove them and I'd have a plate fitted with false teeth, so I was really pleased.

I regret it now though as unquestionably, when Jodi arrived on the scene he had a substantial amount of mercury already inside him. At that stage of his development it wouldn't have been able to pass through his system.

Of course I didn't know that then.

Anyway, you know I had mercury toxicity, but what I don't know is how long the mercury from my amalgam fillings had been leaking.

I had some done when I was a teenager and distinctly remember when I was working in a bank during my early twenties; I had a period where I suffered severe headaches, visual disturbances and my left arm felt numb.

This was around the time I had some dental work done, although I didn't make any connection then. It's quite possible, therefore, my teeth have been leaking for years.

If that were the case, then Daryl too would have been born with mercury in his system, though not as much as Jodi because I didn't have any dental work done whilst pregnant with him.

However, I did breastfeed both children, Daryl for nine months and Jodi for five and a half months and mercury can also be passed through breast milk.

Jodi and I have the same blood group, 'O' rhesus negative, but Daryl and Malcolm are 'O' rhesus positive.

This meant soon after Daryl was born I was given an Anti-D vaccine to prevent problems developing in subsequent pregnancies and that apparently also contains mercury.

Of course that wouldn't necessarily have affected Jodi too much in terms of mercury, but it could have Daryl as I was breastfeeding him.

When they were tested, the levels of mercury in both Daryl and Jodi were as high as mine, but clearly they couldn't have received all of it from me, so where did it come from?

Neither of them had ever had any fillings so another route could be childhood vaccines.

Now I don't know how many people just go along to the doctors and have an injection when they're told to without ever thinking about why they're having it, or indeed what's in it, but I was one of them.

I considered myself to be a conscientious parent and had my children inoculated as and when required.

Of course I checked for any obvious signs of them being unwell at the time, but if there was something going on inside, how could I possibly know?

The theory behind vaccines is if you put a weakened version of a live vaccine into someone, then that person's immune system will send out antibodies to fight against it.

Hopefully, after a bit of a tussle, the antibodies win. They then remember what their foe was like, and if the same nasty ever attacks again in its full strength, they'll be ready to deal with it.

Sounds good doesn't it?

The problem is vaccines are made up of a weakened live virus, which is then strengthened with antibody boosters and stabilizers.

I've read all sorts of incredible things are added, such as: neomycin, streptomycin, sodium chloride, sodium hydroxide, aluminium hydroxide, aluminium hydrochloride, sorbitol, hydrolized gelatin, formaldehyde, and thimerosal, (a mercury derivative).

No doubt you've heard of formaldehyde as it's used for embalming bodies, but it's also an extremely toxic substance, as is aluminium, and mercury, (which is contained in thimerosal).

All of them are found in childhood vaccines, and are injected directly into the blood stream of supposedly healthy babies, thereby avoiding the body's initial barriers of defence, i.e. skin and mucous substances in the nose and throat.

Another thing to consider, apart from the things we know to be in the vaccines, are the things we don't know are in them. I've read about incidences of vaccines being contaminated by undetected animal viruses passed on when the original "live" virus was weakened.

In the 1950's and 1960's, millions of people were given contaminated polio vaccines, apparently due to the monkey organs used to make it.

That's what I've read anyway and I'm sure it must be true otherwise the person who wrote it and his publishers would have been sued.

It's the type of story certain people prefer to keep hushed up and that's understandable - just like the version of MMR containing the Urabe 9 mumps vaccine, which was quietly withdrawn in 1992 after three years because of the danger of aseptic meningitis.

Vaccines have been developed to eradicate preventable communicable diseases and they do a very good job so anything that deters people from having them is not good for the medical profession – or the drug manufacturers.

It's a big and lucrative business, but I think people ought to be advised of the contraindications of each one before they have them so they can make an informed choice as to whether they wish to go ahead or not.

The problem governments face though is that policies are made for the interest of the wider population and clearly one hat doesn't fit everyone.

Health authorities have repeatedly assured us vaccines are the way to go to prevent communicable diseases and are safe for the majority of people, but it’s those in the minority who pay the price if they aren’t.

If it's ever proven a vaccine, or any of its components have caused disabilities like autism, it could make the general public distrust any of their recommendations, so that's a major consideration.

In the papers and the news we now often hear about Gulf War Syndrome and the debilitating health issues suffered by those who received a cocktail of vaccines before going out to serve their country.

Lots of research has been done apparently, but nothing has yet been proven, which doesn't come as a surprise.

Now in UK, another set of individuals are questioning the Hep B vaccines they were given in order to work in health care, and a group of them are considering possible litigation, either against the NHS or the drug manufacturers.

Many health care workers have seen their health deteriorate so much since having the Hep B vaccine they've had to give up work. Currently they can’t claim compensation because Hep B is not on the list “proven” to cause adverse vaccine damage.

However, a new European Consensus ruling has meant the Hep B booster is now given to health care workers after 15 years instead of 5 years. That's a considerably increased gap for something supposedly safe, don’t you think?

I know someone who had her booster 2 years after her original Hep B vaccines and she can no longer work.

Zoe's symptoms are similar to those of multiple sclerosis, but as that's not the cause her doctors wanted to send her down the mental illness route. They aren't too keen to accept the notion she may have vaccine damage.

She's as sane as anyone though and her symptoms are very real, just like all the thousands of other people belonging to vaccine support groups.

Currently she has a diagnosis of Chronic Fatigue Syndrome/ME and in a book entitled "What Doctors Don't Tell You" by Lynne McTaggart, it says that CFS/ME could possibly be caused by mercury and vaccinations.

After I joined Pam Clayton's mercury helpline, I was invited to send a letter or e-mail to the UK National Audit Office. They were considering the possibility of a study on NHS dental services because of the problems associated with the use of mercury amalgam.

I duly sent off a letter, as did thousands of other people. In fact the Audit Office was inundated with mail and couldn't get on with their regular work.

I got to read some of those letters myself and realised the extent of the problems mercury can cause. One of the letters though was from Professor Boyd Haley, who is currently the Professor and Chair at the Department of Chemistry in the University of Kentucky and one of Americas leading mercury scientists.

He'd published an article entitled: "The Relationship of the Toxic Effects of Mercury to Exacerbation of the Medical Condition Classified as Alzheimer's Disease".

I read it, or at least I tried to but it was very technical and quite frankly I didn't understand half of it. However, some bits caught my attention, specifically those to do with thimerosal.

I sat down and e-mailed Professor Haley to ask if he would kindly explain them to me in simple language. Surprisingly he replied almost immediately, so, "Thank you Professor Haley".

It seems thimerosal or thiomersal as you sometimes see it written, is a mercury-based derivative used as a preservative in most childhood vaccines and has been around for over seventy years.

There seems to be little evidence it was ever properly tested for safety, but it's efficient for the purpose, so was used.

Amazingly, in USA it was banned from vaccines for dogs in 1992 and has been banned from childhood vaccines over there, since March 2002. Certain states actively tried to reduce it from as early as 1999.

It's still used in vaccines over here in the UK however, and it's the government's policy at the moment to continue to do so. They are supposed to be phasing it out though.

An article in the Lancet (medical journal) recently challenged the usual health authority mantra that "there is no conclusive evidence that points to a link between thimerosal and ill health" by pointing out no thorough, systematic study had ever proven the safety of it either!

Thimerosal is 49.6% mercury by weight and this is what Professor Haley has to say on the subject. I'm using his words with his agreement because they are self-explanatory.

Also, as they are in simplified English for my benefit, I may give out the wrong information if I try to simplify them even more : -

"Thimerosal concentrations in vaccines is about 125,000 nanomolar and 10 nanomolar causes significant neuron death in cultured nerve cells. This is with pure thimerosal.

If one also adds aluminium or testosterone, the amount of thimerosal needed to cause neuron death is decreased. That is, the thimerosal is more toxic in the presence of these compounds.

In fact, thimerosal concentrations that kill less than 2 – 3% of neurons at 3 hours will kill 100% if very low (and completely non-toxic) levels of testosterone are present.

I have been told that mothers of autistic children had higher levels of testosterone in their amniotic fluid when compared to appropriate controls, and there are also likely other genetic susceptibility factors that place children at risk to mercury exposure.

There is no doubt that mercury from a mother's amalgam is transferred to the foetus. Mercury and thimerosal (ethyl-mercury) are both toxic to the same nervous system proteins, therefore, their toxicities would be additive at the least.

It is likely that the effect of thimerosal on nervous system neurons is greatly different for different children. All my research says is that thimerosal is a very possible cause of autism since it is

1) injected into infants,

2) very neurotoxic and

3) has toxicity enhancement by testosterone that may explain why boys get the disease at a 4:1 ratio to girls.

The brain is loaded with neurons and some new research indicates that the injured brain can somewhat be repaired with proper treatments.

In autism, you do not have to kill many neurons, if any. You need just to disrupt neuronal development at a stage that impairs the function of speech development and certain cognitive abilities.

It is plausible that thimerosal does this as it is the only toxin (excluding that introduced through the mother as through her amalgams) we can identify, that infants are exposed to that they were not exposed to before the epidemic of "regressive" autism."

Now do you see where I'm leading?

My teeth were leaking mercury, my hormones were disrupted and my testosterone levels were high which explained my continual trips to the electrolysis clinic, and then I zapped Jodi with thimerosal.

It's no wonder he flipped eventually.

You see I'm totally convinced he didn't always have autism, as you'll know if you read his first book, (and if you haven't, I ask again, why not)?

Jodi had all his required injections at the appropriate times and by the time he was six months old had received his BCG, (which is not given until between 10 and 13 years of age in developed countries such as UK where there is less risk of tuberculosis); Hepatitis B1, B2, B3 containing aluminium hydroxide, thimerosal, and formaldehyde (and again only given in countries where there is a high risk of hepatitis B); three lots of Diptheria, Tetanus and Pertussis (whooping cough) containing thimerosal; and three lots of Polio containing formaldehyde.

That's a lot of toxic substances for a developing baby, but apart from the occasional red mark he didn't appear to suffer any ill effects.

He didn't actually display any autistic traits until after the MMR injection. That appears to be quite common in a lot of cases of what is termed "regressive autism".

Naturally people wonder why, and ask what the possible connection could be - I did.

The MMR, (Measles, Mumps and Rubella) vaccine contains live measles and live mumps virus grown in cell cultures of chick embryo, live rubella virus grown in human diploid cell culture (aborted human foetus), neomycin (an antibiotic), sorbitol, and hydrolized gelatin. It doesn't contain thimerosal.

Some of the guidelines for its use, apart from the obvious fact the child should be healthy, is that the child should not react severely to neomycin or kanamycin, have hypersensitivity to any component of MMR including gelatine, have febrile respiratory illness or have untreated malignant diseases or altered immunity.

I find that last bit very interesting.

How would you know without testing?

There are a lot of people now demanding at the very least a questionnaire be completed before any child receives the MMR as a screening process for any contraindications that might suggest possible vaccine damage.

Of course that wouldn't necessarily guarantee a child's safety – nothing can, but it might help. Questions like –

* Is the child allergic to eggs?

* Has the child been unwell in the last few days?

* What is the family health history?

* Did the child have any adverse vaccine reactions following previous injections?

All I was asked was whether Jodi was well and if he had a temperature.

He was and he didn't.

Look what happened.

No one asked about the febrile convulsions he had when he was ten months old although they were on his medical records.

The MMR is a contentious issue and there will always be two different opinions as to whether or not it does contribute to autism.

My own opinion is in certain cases it most definitely does and I'm now convinced Jodi is one of them. It seems the measles part of the MMR attacks the immune system so if a child has already been compromised, I think it could just be enough to tip the balance.

There has been speculation the MMR wasn't properly tested before it was introduced into the UK in 1988, and an article which appeared in the Sunday Herald in December, 2000 said several senior clinicians, including a former senior professional medical officer at the UK Department of Health, felt the decision to license it was premature because there was insufficient evidence of its safety.

So why did it get a license?

Well, some cynics say it was because one third of the members of the British government committee that advised on the safety of the MMR vaccine supposedly had financial interests in the drug companies that made the treatment.

The Sunday Times printed an article in January 2001 suggesting twelve of the thirty-six members of the British Committee on Safety of Medicines had financial links with the MMR manufacturers, whose products they had given the all-clear on the basis of published research.

Five of them supposedly held shares in the drug companies, or were paid consultants, whilst the other seven had received grants or sponsorships from them to fund academic studies or clinical trials.

If true, that smacks to me a bit of, "it's not what you know but whom you know". The Daily Mail also ran an interesting article about the MMR over a three-day period in March 2003 revealing the same information as the Sunday Times, and more.

Worrying isn't it?

I don't know if it is true or not but I've also read, (and I can't remember where), that extensive tests weren't actually done on the MMR vaccine because the single vaccines for the viruses had previously been used successfully.

It was felt, therefore, as each component had a proven individual track record, it would be safe and more cost effective in terms of time and money to just combine the three.

We're told Safety Data tests for the MMR were carried out for up for sixty-three days, which doesn't seem very long to me, but apparently six weeks is normal for vaccines.

Parents involved in the MMR trials were asked to report any significant illnesses, but late onset autism doesn't always reveal itself immediately and anyway, from my experience the symptoms, which form part of a gradual process, would not be considered a "significant illness".

Autism is a multi-factorial disorder and affects each unique individual differently.

In Jodi's case the first sign was him banging his head against shopping trolley handles, walls and the floor.

He became miserable and developed a series of ear infections but the doctors just said he was probably teething and gave him antibiotics.

You see although now those symptoms might ring a few alarm bells, back in 1990 two years after the introduction of the MMR the statistics showing the rise in autism hadn't materialised.

He later went on to lose all his social and language skills, but it certainly took longer than sixty- three days, so even if we'd been part of the trials I doubt I'd have noted any "significant illness" – just weird and unusual behaviour.

Although national safety regulations require all side effects to be reported it doesn't mean they actually were, especially when you consider the type of changes parents report in the children who go on to develop autism didn't receive any publicity until 1997 – nine years after the introduction of the MMR and the safety tests.

Anyway, it's government policy the MMR vaccine is safe and regularly we hear of surveys confirming this opinion. As general reviews on the MMR have failed to find a link between MMR and autism, the Department of Health has taken this to mean there is no link.

Doctors receive a financial bonus for achieving take up targets for vaccines, which I'm told is not on a pro-rata sliding scale so there must be enormous pressure on them to recommend the MMR vaccination.

I feel sorry for them as I'm sure some doctors must have doubts, which they're unable to voice, unless of course they want a change of profession!

It's very difficult to get the single vaccines these days although when the MMR was introduced in 1988, the pamphlet which accompanied its introduction in UK, "Immunisation Against Infectious Diseases" stated if parents refused to give their children the combined MMR then single vaccines would be available.

Some parents find this no longer holds true with their local health service though and are willing to travel long distances and pay lots of money to find them.

They believe God gave them their children to cherish, and parents, and not the government, have the right to decide which way is best to look after them.

I think the choice of single or triple vaccines should be made available to all as was originally proposed when the MMR was first introduced. That way parents are in control.

Costs shouldn't come into it but inevitably they do.

In Scotland parents can apparently choose the single option but very few realise it. It's not something widely broadcast, as the health authorities advocate the triple vaccine is best. One thing everyone does agree on though is the long-term financial cost to all the services involved if a child develops autism is immense.

In June 2000 a study for the UK Mental Health Foundation estimated the lifetime costs for a severely autistic individual would amount to almost £3 million.

That sounds incredible but autists generally live to a normal age so all the extra health costs, care costs, special education and transport costs, all add up.

You also have to consider the lost earnings and tax revenue from the autistic person and the relative who'll most likely be looking after him or her.

As a full time carer, I certainly haven't been as productive as I'm sure I could have been had Jodi not developed autism. That's just the financial side of things though.

You can't put a price on the loss of quality of life to all involved. It's immeasurable!

But back now to why I think Jodi became autistic.

This is only my opinion you must understand and I'm not a specialist in this field. I'm just a mother and a housewife, or as I once read, a Research Associate in the field of Child Development and Human Relations and Director of Household Management.

That sounds much more impressive and just as demanding.

Anyone who gets a virus, naturally or otherwise (i.e. vaccines) has the best chance of combating it if they have a good immune system.

Now bearing in mind mercury plays havoc with the immune system, and Jodi almost certainly had plenty inside him by the time he received the MMR, it's fair to say whilst outwardly he appeared okay, inwardly he was most likely not in peak condition.

He may have had the "altered immunity" which should have prevented him having the MMR but at the ripe old age of twelve months and one week he was faced with not one, but three live viruses, all demanding his antibodies come out to fight.

I think a big battle ensued inside him, which just proved too much for his tiny body. Almost immediately strange symptoms began to appear. He lost his social skills, learned behaviour and any language he'd previously demonstrated, and was finally diagnosed with autism some three and a half years later.

Does that make sense to you? It certainly does to me especially in the light of my earlier discoveries.

Incidentally, I've also read the MMR was banned in Japan in 1993 after a record number of children developed adverse reactions.

I found that interesting too because in Japan they eat a lot of fish and shellfish. It's an area renowned for its tuna and that's supposedly another source of mercury.

The larger predatory fish at the top of the food chain, like tuna and swordfish are particularly high risk foods apparently. That's because they eat so many of the smaller fish who feed in the polluted waters.

It's interesting too in the UK, pregnant women are now advised to limit the amount of tuna they eat. (Are the powers that be finally taking the possible mercury connection seriously?)

Leo Kanner was the first person to ever mention autism. He was an experienced child psychologist and late in the 1930's he began to notice a type of child who'd never been described before.

In 1943 he published a paper, which said, "Since 1938, there have come to attention a number of children whose condition differs so markedly and uniquely from anything reported so far, that each case merits a detailed consideration of its fascinating peculiarities".

All these children had been born in the 1930's, and thimerosal was introduced as a preservative for vaccines in the 1930's.

Are you thinking along the same lines as me?

The DTP vaccine was introduced in 1957 and used to be the only childhood vaccine given. Autism then was quite rare and most cases were the classical ones from birth.

Gradually the UK's immunisation schedule expanded and autism is now quite common with many cases being of the late-onset type.

Below is the vaccine schedule recommended for children under the age of three years, which apparently gives the best chance of developing immunity and minimising the risk of them catching the diseases.

You'll see how it has changed over the years.

1968

6 months	Polio, DPT
7 1/2 months	Polio, DPT

1988

3 months	Polio, DPT
5 months	DPT
13 months +	MMR

1996

2 months	Polio, DPT/HIB
3 months	Polio, DPT/HIB
4 months	Polio, DPT/HIB
13 months +	MMR

I was born in 1955, so when I was a child we didn't have that vaccine schedule. It was an accepted fact of life children could, and most likely, would, catch measles, mumps and chickenpox.

Of course it was inconvenient and uncomfortable at the time, but it was reasoned it was better to have these illnesses as a child than as an adult.

We all caught them naturally and I can't think of anyone I know who suffered any long-term side effects because of them, and certainly no one who actually died.

Undoubtedly, there will be some and I don't want to sound dismissive of them, but I personally don't know of any, and until Jodi developed autism, I'd never heard of it so obviously none of my peers suffered from that disability either.

However, I now know of several children who caught measles and chickenpox even after receiving the MMR vaccination and thousands of children who developed delayed autism. Jodi is one of them.

I've done a lot of research and I'm definitely not the only one who thinks it coincidental the amount of children diagnosed with bowel problems, and/or falling under the autistic spectrum, has increased with the introduction of more and more recommended childhood vaccines, and specifically since the MMR was introduced in 1988.

There are numerous web sites dealing with the same subject, but one of the most enlightening is probably www.autismuk.com.

Another you can log on to is hosted and maintained by The Healing Centre On-Line, where I found an article on web page http//www.healing-arts.org/children/main.htm, entitled, "Mercury from Thimerosal in Vaccines Linked to Increase in Autism in Confidential CDC Study".

It said mercury from thimerosal in vaccines was linked to a marked increase in autism and exposure to more than 62.5 micrograms of mercury within the first three months of life significantly increases a child's risk of developing neurodevelopmental disorders such as speech and language delay, autism, stuttering and attention deficit disorder.

I also found on the Autism Research Institute web site under http//www.autism.com/ari/mercury/long.html, a very interesting article that said the characteristics of autism and mercury poisoning (HgP) are so similar as to suggest many cases of autism are a form of mercury poisoning. It said for these children, the exposure route is childhood vaccines, most of which contain thimerosal.

It detailed the quantities injected during the various vaccines and by the time a child born in the USA in the 1990's was two years old, it would typically receive 237.5 micrograms.

According to the article the child would have had 75 micrograms by the time it was 2 months old. It said if this vaccinal mercury wasn't excreted it migrates to the brain.

Makes you think doesn't it?

Jodi was born in Brunei in 1989 and had all his injections when I was told he required them. I used to take him along to the clinic where the Chinese and Malay nurses would check his weight and ask me if he was okay.

We'd sit in the hot waiting room under the ceiling fan, wearing as few clothes as possible, and I'd check for obvious outward signs of illness.

Jodi was always the centre of attention as he was a big baby compared with the locals, very happy and sociable, and, of course, he was white, which was a bit of a novelty out there at the time.

As he always appeared to be fine, he received his HEP B1 at one day old, BCG at three and a half weeks, HEP B2 at 1 month, DPT and Polio at 3, 4,and 5 month intervals, HEP B3 at 6 months and his MMR at one year and one week.

Brunei as you may know is in Borneo, just off the equator. There are no real seasons although you supposedly get a wet and dry one each year.

It's hot and humid every day, and Brunei's claim to fame is lots of jungle and oil. The Sultan is purportedly the richest man in the world.

I'm told, (although I can't confirm this), because it's such a hot country, more preservative is required in the vaccines over there. If that's the case, when Jodi had his injections, it's just possible he received even more thimerosal than is normally recommended.

I don't know, but any ethyl mercury from the thimerosal, added to the mercury already in his system from my dental amalgam, mixed up with a bit of aluminium, formaldehyde from vaccines and our combined testosterone was likely stirring up a heady brew inside him, wouldn't you agree?

Do you think just maybe his immune system was taking a bit of a pounding?

I went on to check the similarities between mercury toxicity and autism and found a two columned table entitled, "Summary Comparison of Characteristics of Autism and Mercury Poisoning" on the Autism Research Institute website.

It was compiled by Sallie Bernard and others and is quite a revelation in terms of the similarities between the two topics. It listed the various, characteristics under -

* Psychiatric Disturbances,
* Speech, Language and Hearing Deficits,
* Sensory Abnormalities,
* Cognitive Impairments,
* Unusual Behaviours,
* Physical Disturbances,
* Abnormal Biochemistry,
* Immune Dysfunction,
* CNS Structural Pathology,
* Abnormalities in Neuro-chemistry,
* EEG Abnormalities/Epilepsy
* Population Characteristics,

Amazingly both the Mercury Poisoning and the Autism sides of the table were virtually the same.

It was almost like looking at a reflection in a mirror.

Even a quick glance shows how plausible the earlier suggestion of autism being a form of mercury poisoning is.

I don't want you to just take my word for it though, so if you have access to a computer and are even slightly intrigued I suggest you check it out for yourself.

So there you have it. Now you know why I think Jodi has autism and you'll have to make your own mind up whether you think I could be right or not.

It would be nice if it were that simple and something could be done for future generations. Clearly it's too late for Jodi.

All the indications are the combination of mercury, formaldehyde, aluminium and testosterone affected the neurons in his brain at a crucial stage in his development and I'm doubtful they can ever be repaired.

We continue to try anything that might help him though.

In a weird sort of way, if mercury is the key, then autism, like so many other illnesses in our civilised society is sort of self-inflicted. Of course I don't mean we deliberately go out and make ourselves ill, but we don't seem to have a lot of choice.

People say you are what you eat and certainly what we put into our bodies appears to be playing a major part in our health.

My generation is not as strong as my parents, and they're not as robust as their forebears. Okay, we live longer but we suffer from all sorts of ailments relatively unheard of a few years ago.

I wonder sometimes whether we rely on too many drugs and whether that's because of who funds the training of the medical experts who prescribe them?

I just don't know but apparently when doctors go to medical school, nutrition plays very little, if any, in the coursework covered.

That's really sad considering everyone knows we benefit from a healthy diet. Admittedly most doctors will ask you if you're eating enough fruit and vegetables but that's about as far as it goes.

Here's me talking like an expert and I'm pathetic in the kitchen and despite my best intentions, Jodi's diet is lousy, although in my defence that is mostly his fault.

His diet is self-restricted – very!

These days though, even if you were to eat all the meat, fruit and vegetables you're supposed to, it's highly unlikely you'd get all the minerals and vitamins you need.

The soil is depleted from all the natural ones and replaced with goodness knows what.

Organic foods are supposedly much safer and healthier but no matter how good the food is, if your body can't absorb the different minerals then for all nutritional intents and purposes it's useless.

Harmful chemicals and toxins are everywhere and if they aren't sprayed or injected into your food then they'll be in the packaging.

You can find them in cosmetics, medications, household and garden chemicals and they're used in numerous industrial processes.

Many ailments are put down to old age and are supposed to be an accepted part of life. My dad has suffered from arthritis for years and it's reached the stage where it can reduce him to tears sometimes.

The doctors say there's nothing they can do.

He's in his seventies and yet there are some remote places in the world where people have been known to live until they're well over 100 years old, with some even surviving until 150 and beyond.

Apparently some of the men have even fathered children when they'd passed the age where they'd receive a congratulatory telegram from the Queen in this country.

Now that conjures up all sorts of images and puts a whole new slant on the phrase, "grab a granny".

The Hunza people live in the remote Himalayan foothills of North-eastern Pakistan. When they were discovered in the late 1920's they didn't suffer from any of the illnesses we do, so arthritis, which so many people suffer from, can't just be an accepted symptom of old age, can it?

It appears, their teeth were in the finest condition and they were physically and mentally healthy with no sign of cancer, heart disease, diabetes, ulcers, colitis, diverticulosis, high blood pressure or childhood ailments.

What does that tell you?

Also, there was no sign of juvenile delinquency or crime so they must have been doing something right. I mention that because I've read somewhere there's some evidence rape and murder became more prevalent after the introduction of more copper in dental amalgam.

I can't comment on that. It sounds a bit extreme to me but judging from the crime figures these days, something clearly went wrong somewhere.

I just hope, whatever it was, doesn't spread to the remote Himalayan foothills of North-eastern Pakistan where you can still meet wrinkled folk claiming to be more than one hundred years old. They insist their longevity and good health is due to good soil and a frugal diet.

Well, I did say I'd be taking you on a scenic route and I certainly have. Hope you haven't been too confused?

I still haven't finished though as I want to get back to Jodi and show just how much progress he's made in the past twelve months.

After his de-tox Jodi had a second electro-dermal screening test and all his heavy metal levels had dropped dramatically.

They are now in a weakened state and should hopefully not cause him further problems, but as there are toxins everywhere I had planned to follow the programme at least once a year.

I've recently learned though because of the way the autists stomach works, or doesn't as the case may be, it might be better to de-tox him again and then give him one or two capsules every week to keep the toxins at bay, so that's what I'm doing.

I noticed considerable improvements in him during, after and since the first course and I guess I'm hoping the more I do it, the more I'll see.

I don't know if it will work like that but as the Humet®-R is a health supplement anyway I have no qualms about it causing him harm.

He still follows a nutritional programme involving taking extra vitamins and supplements and his overall health has improved. He used to suffer from dandruff, dry, irritating skin on the soles of his feet, and intolerance to gluten products, but seems fine now.

He hated the texture of soap but tolerates it now by using a scrunchie, and will even allow us to shave him with proper foam and a razor.

We have to put a small amount of foam on his face, shave it off and then move on to another bit. I don't think he really likes it but will nevertheless tell us if we miss a bit.

I'm sure the fact he's seen a barber shave a customer in one of his Thomas the Tank videos has helped overcome this hurdle.

He communicates more now and actually wants to. I'm not saying he always uses words. Frequently he uses mime to convey his message but it's equally effective.

Only last week he came to me, waved his hands around a few times like some rich person dismissing a servant and said "please, please".

He then mimed wiping something up before taking hold of my hand and leading me to the utility room where I found two broken eggs on the floor.

They'd dropped out of the compartment in the fridge door when he'd gone to get his apple drink.

The next day, he did the same thing but this time when he said, “please, please”, I asked him what he wanted and he replied, “open curtains” because I’d neglected to pull them back.

I wonder if I’d held out the day before, whether he would have said “eggs, broken” as I know he can say and understands both words.

I’m not sure about language though and the jury is still out as to whether I really want him to speak properly. I have this fear if he says lots of words, people will expect too much from him.

Sometimes he does use simple language and that pleases me enormously even though he often gets it muddled up. For instance, when he wants the cover straightened on his bed he’ll say, “push”, when he means, “pull”.

I suppose it’s because if he were moving the duvet in the direction he wants it to go then he would be pushing it.

Also, when he wants to show me something he’ll say, “I’m coming” rather than “come and look at this”, and today he said to me, “I’ll take you”.

When I asked him where he wanted to go, he replied, “grandma, grandad” which was obviously his way of telling me he wanted to visit my parents.

Naturally we went.

It's amazing when he responds to questions I ask him too, albeit very simply. He's just been for an overnight stay at respite care and now when he goes I have to tell him not just the day I am picking him up, but the time as well.

On one particular occasion I told him I'd be collecting him on Thursday morning "after breakfast".

On the way home in the car he told me "Thursday morning, after breakfast, mummy coming – Jodi". When I asked him what he'd had for breakfast he told me "cornflakes".

With further questioning I learned he'd had a "blue and white dish", used a "spoon", and had "blackcurrant" to drink.

As I drove home my eyes were glazed over for a while so it's probably just as well the country roads were very quiet.

He reads to me more now and I know he now realises that words actually relate to something. He comes to get me every time the title of a new episode comes up on the television screen when he's watching a video because he wants to know what it says.

I tell him and he repeats it with a look on his face I can only describe as satisfaction.

He's also made me type out the words to every single Spot episode so when he watches those videos, he can follow the stories with his finger and read the words.

It took me ages, especially as the video was playing and I was expected to listen to the story, type it out, look at Jodi narrating the words and say the story too.

He'd get hold of my chin and move it up and down like a ventriloquist's dummy trying to get me to say the right words, not realising how bad my memory is compared to his.

I'm not the fastest or most accurate of typists so missed words out, and got some wrong but afterwards Jodi always corrected me.

This wonderful child, who supposedly can't read, knew exactly when I'd typed something wrong and would point to it on the screen and tell me what it should have been.

Even so, I still made mistakes and now, when he reads along to the episodes, he always knows where I've gone wrong and his finger pauses at an error, or comes completely off the sheet if I've missed something out.

He never ceases to amaze me.

It's that way for other people too, and one of the learning support assistants at his school has confessed that working with Jodi has made her throw all her preconceived ideas about autism out of the window.

His teacher had to revise the work she had planned for him at the beginning of term because it was proving too easy. She's amazed how much he understands.

His writing has improved tremendously and if he wants to write something down and can't spell it he'll say the word and look at me until I tell him.

Mostly he just writes out the titles of his videos but it doesn't matter because it's helping his spelling, writing and reading abilities.

He decided he wanted a certain video about steam trains at the end of last year and wrote its title on every calendar in the house, including the one in Daryl's room.

He wasn't too pleased especially as it was an old video and difficult to locate. As it took a long time to find, Jodi wrote the title of the video on every calendar, every weekend for months, and even wrote "red box" just to make sure there were no mistakes.

Daryl was delighted when we managed to get a copy but not as much as Jodi!

You know sometimes I even forget he has a disability.

Recently, I took him bowling to the same place he went on his thirteenth birthday. It was noisy and crowded but he was fine about it all.

Much to my amazement he bowled one handed just like everyone else, and won. You can imagine how well that went down with Daryl, but if it hadn't been for the fact Jodi had his finger in his ear throughout the whole session, one could be forgiven for thinking he was just like all the other children there.

He's certainly more observant now so maybe he's decided he wants to be like them, which is why he's changed his bowling style.

Clearly he's made great progress since the beginning of school term and at Christmas was selected to be a shepherd in the nativity play held in Ely Cathedral.

I felt so proud, especially as he performed his part beautifully and didn't test the sound effects by stamping on the floor that time!

His school has just performed their own version of Supercalifragalisticexpialidocious from Mary Poppins and every child in the school was involved regardless of their disability.

It was incredibly moving and I don't think there was a dry eye in the hall.

Jodi was amazing in his role. His timing was perfect and the head mistress remarked to me on how confident Jodi has become.

On Boxing Day he attended a family party and joined in beautifully. He wasn't at all fazed by the fact there were eighteen noisy people in one house and it was the first time ever I hadn't felt the need to leave long before everyone else did.

My parents celebrated their Golden Wedding recently and had a big party with about 150 guests. They hired a hall with music. Jodi was the first on the dance floor and didn't stand out in the crowd.

He even got up and danced with my mum's cousin. Olive was amazed, as he doesn't really know her. She said it made her night.

You may recall shopping for shoes used to be an absolute nightmare as far as Jodi was concerned.

He wouldn't let anyone measure his feet and would only have shoes that were just like the ones he already had, but during the January sales, we all went looking for trainers for Malcolm and Daryl.

The two older Shaw's chose some to fit on and whilst I was looking at the ladies selection, Jodi must have decided he would have a pair too.

He was sitting down fitting some on before I even realised. They were three sizes too big and still had the paper stuffed in the end of the toes but he obviously liked them so we got him a pair in his correct size.

It was the easiest shoe shopping experience with him I've ever had.

A week later, Malcolm decided to buy some more formal shoes and once again Jodi took a pair of shoes from the shelf. I was dreading he was going to start collecting them the way he had his videos, but infact he had selected them for his dad and wanted to sort out the laces.

The shop assistant jokingly offered him a job!

Jodi no longer eats his toenails. You may remember he considered them a delicacy and were worried when he pulled them because his toes looked really red and painful sometimes.

On one occasion I was concerned he had an in growing toenail but felt sure he'd never let a chiropodist do anything about it.

I put Savlon cream on it but when Jodi's review came up with his school paediatrician I got him to have a look.

Jodi dutifully took off his sock and shoe to show the doctor and as he knelt down to examine his foot; Jodi tapped him on the shoulder, said "cream" and rapidly put his sock back on.

The paediatrician referred us to a chiropodist who said it was unlikely Jodi would let him carry out any treatment. He suggested we try putting Tea Tree Oil on which might help.

I bought some and dabbed it on Jodi's toe with a cotton bud. I only did it once before he took over and did it himself. He put it on every nail on both feet but I didn't mind.

For a while his toes look very healthy but then he decided to cut his nails himself with scissors. He got a bit carried away and the result was a trip to the hospital to have two in growing toenails sorted under general anaesthetic.

Again he was brilliant though and amazed everyone by ripping off the dressings almost before we'd got home from the hospital and dressed them again himself.

He didn't seem to feel any pain at all and certainly didn't demand any sympathy.

I sometimes wonder why Jodi used to eat his toenails. All autists do things for a reason so could he have known his body was lacking in minerals and was doing his bit towards re-cycling?

Clearly Jodi still has problems with his hearing and can tolerate some things really loud but not others. Even some relatively quiet noises seem to bother him.

He spends a lot of time with his finger in his ear, like at the bowling alley, or will put his hands over both ears if a motorbike, lorry or 'plane go by.

Often he puts his left arm over his head so that his left hand covers his right ear and the top of his left arm covers his left ear. I've not yet worked out why he does that, as his right hand is generally free at the time.

The ear thing gets him noticed though and he does tend to stand out a bit. We were in the chemist the other day and had to queue to see the pharmacist.

As it was half term there were a lot of children with their mothers. Initially, Jodi looked like any other teenage boy but then he started to tell a story repeating the same phrases over and over again until he was happy they sounded correct.

He had his finger in his ear the whole time, which I suspect was to block out some of the background noise so he could concentrate on the story he was attempting to relate.

He also stamped his foot when he got stuck on a word as if it would suddenly send the phrase shooting up his body and out of his mouth.

Children openly stared trying to work him out, and parents gave sideways glances, not really wanting to be obvious but unable to resist. I just smiled and said "Incase you're wondering, he's autistic" and gave him a cuddle as he sniffed my hair.

There was one young woman queuing, clearly at an age with no responsibilities and very few cares in the world, who was obviously bothered by Jodi repeating his phrases over and over. I can almost be certain what she was thinking and I advise her to take care.

You see I remember a trip to a swimming pool long ago when Malcolm and I were living in Brunei before we had children of our own.

We were with some friends relaxing by the baby pool as they had small children at the time.

Close to us were a family with two children; a boy and a girl.

The older boy was walking around energetically relating a story in a very loud, monotone voice to no one in particular. His parents certainly weren't listening and his little sister kept looking up at the sky repeating, "helicopter, helicopter", over and over and over again.

I distinctly remember after what seemed like hearing it for the hundredth time Malcolm got really annoyed and hissed, "Shut that bloody kid up".

I'm not sure whether the parents heard it or not as they appeared to be oblivious to what was going on around them.

Our friends knew of the boy from school and it seems he was incredibly intelligent but naughty. There was speculation the work in school was just too easy for him but no one thought there was anything seriously wrong, as he looked okay.

On reflection, it's most likely the boy had Asperger's Syndrome and his little sister, autism, and I often wonder whether we were given Jodi to teach us tolerance and understanding.

It's worked and just like the parents mentioned above, I too have discovered the art of just switching off.

One thing Jodi does like loud and doesn't cover his ears for is his Fantasia music CD. He loves it and plays it every time we go in the car.

When Malcolm heard Jodi listen to it for the first time last summer, he expressed surprise he liked classical music. Daryl retorted it wasn't classical music - it was Disney. He's right of course because whenever Jodi listens to it, he performs the appropriate animated movement sequences that go with the music in the film.

His favourite is "The Sorcerer's Apprentice" and it's hilarious to watch him pretend to be the broom carrying and emptying the water, or being the Sorcerer waving his wand, especially when he's strapped in the back seat of the car.

He also sings along beautifully to Ave Maria in Italian but I don't suppose languages make any difference to him. He just repeats what he hears and most likely doesn't consider the meaning.

I'm convinced his mind must now be clearer. I know the difference the removal of heavy metals made to me.

You only have to consider last year I couldn't remember why I was going from one room to another, and now with help from Jodi, I've almost finished this story.

Today is just one example of how far he's come.

This morning I telephoned a friend as we'd arranged for her to ring me at a certain time and as Daryl wanted me to take him to meet his friends, it meant I wouldn't be here.

She was out though so I left a message on her answer phone.

It was a nice morning and I had a lot of washing to hang out before we left in the car, so I told Jodi to clean his teeth and put his shoes on whilst Daryl and I hung the clothes out.

We went outside, leaving Jodi to get ready, expecting him to appear long before our task had been finished, but he didn't.

When I came into the house to see what was taking him so long and to ask if he was ready, he waved his hand and said, "telephone".

I rang 1471 and discovered my friend had rung back so I gave her a quick call. It's just as well I did because she was really worried.

Apparently, Jodi had answered the telephone three times. The first time, he'd just said "Hello", the second time he'd had more of a conversation,(at least by his standards), and the third time it was another "Hello".

My friend was concerned something had happened to me and that Jodi was all alone in the house. She was seriously considering either coming over or 'phoning the police.

I hadn't heard the 'phone ring at all and was amazed he'd answered it. What was more amazing though was the way he wouldn't come outside or let me leave to take Daryl to football until he had told me it had rang.

After dropping Daryl off, we went over to see my parents. They weren't in and when Jodi realised the door was locked he said, "Where is everybody?" Good use of language I think you'll agree.

We came home and as we drove back I suggested to Jodi we might wash the car. He was sitting in the back seat listening to Fantasia at the time and the remark was made in casual conversation without me looking at him obviously, as that would have been a bit dangerous.

Anyway, as soon as we got home he took off his best jumper, put on an old coat, got the buckets and sponges from the garage, prepared the water and requested his "boots". He then went outside and proceeded to wash the car, even taking the rubber mats out from inside.

Can you imagine a "normal" teenage child doing that? I suspect all sorts of reminders would be required, no doubt greeted with whinging, whining and demands for payment.

After he'd put the hose away, he took his wet boots off outside, went into the house, stripped off his wet clothes, put them in the washing basket, got himself dressed and when I came in, he handed me a towel as he could see I was a bit wet too.

He's very observant and considerate in so many ways although he probably doesn't even realise it. He puts the washing machine on sometimes especially if I've half loaded it.

He'll put the washing powder and conditioner in, turn the dial to the correct number for a colour wash, switch it on and give the door a hit because our machine is a bit temperamental.

He then takes me to see what he's done and says "Thanks" although in reality that's what I should be saying to him. I'm so glad he didn't watch me use a whites wash otherwise I imagine quite a few clothes would get ruined with the higher temperature!

I know I'm so lucky with him and appreciate how much he's improved. In some ways he is so "normal" and yet in many more he isn't. I worry about the progress he's making though. You see at the moment he's so happy and doesn't appear to know or care that he's different.

What will happen if he ever does?

My other son, Daryl, has control over his own life but can be hurt both physically and emotionally. I worry about him too, but Jodi is currently just at the mercy of how people choose to behave towards him and what sort of life they allow him to have.

I select those people I have around him carefully.

I take him to an evening class once a week where we learn craft skills. So far he has made a felt picture, a mobile, a musical instrument, a puppet, some boxes, a coaster a woven bowl, a mosaic tile, a paper lantern, and a hat out of the sleeve of a jumper.

He seems to enjoy it, especially the tidying up afterwards (and in-between) and everyone just accepts him, which is lovely. It doesn't bother them that he sometimes talks throughout the entire class and says, "No smacking" every time he doesn't want to do something.

He's just Jodi and that's what he does. He seems to be getting more artistic and his painting and colouring have improved immensely. He got a sequin picture for Christmas of a dolphin and slowly and surely he's completing it.

We started it in January and I forgot about it until last week. I couldn't understand why Jodi wouldn't start to do it again as he knew exactly what was required but he just kept holding his index finger and thumb up in a pincer like position and muttering something.

Eventually, he gave up trying to explain what he wanted and went to the sewing box to get a thimble. Obviously he remembered pushing the pins through the sequins and into the felt hurt.

Oh yes, Jodi's Journey is definitely on the right track and I'll do all I can to make sure it stays that way.

Sorry, bet you thought you were finished there, but I promise this is the last section.

I'm sure there'll be some people who've read this book and are now convinced they or someone they know may also have heavy metal toxicity.

That may very well be the case, but if one of them is you, please don't blame your dentists or doctors if they haven't yet picked it up.

It's highly unlikely any of their training would ever have indicated mercury toxicity caused by dental amalgam could be a problem.

As it's not a contagious disease it doesn't have to be recorded so there are no accurate records of just how many people are actually affected.

Also, it's not something which either the dental or health authorities seem to want to consider viable – yet!

Dentists ought to be made aware though as one of the known symptoms of mercury toxicity is suicidal thoughts, and apparently out of all professions, dentistry boasts the highest rate of suicide.

Mercury toxicity isn't easy to test for as the symptoms are vague and can be attributable to many different ailments.

The poor general practitioners have to perform a process of elimination based on the symptoms the patient offers and it's pretty difficult for them.

Don't forget, these symptoms can show up months and even years after any dental work has been done.

The key aspect of mercury toxicity though seems to be an increasing number of inexplicable symptoms.

There's a very cheap and simple test that can be done using saliva and litmus paper, which can determine if you have a heavy metal problem but I don't know of any general practitioners who use it.

It's a pity holistic medicine isn't part of the NHS, but perhaps one day all the different practices will join forces and work as a team instead of competitors.

If the ultimate aim is to make and keep people healthy then it surely shouldn't matter which route is taken to achieve that goal.

I have nothing but praise for the dentists and doctors who always attempted to do what they considered best for me (and Jodi) at the time, but as new information and more awareness of the possible contribution of mercury and nutrition to so many ailments comes to light, I've no doubt both professions will give the matter more thought. I know there's a lot of research going into it concerning autism.

The de-toxification and nutritional protocols Jodi and I followed were recommended by a Natural Health Practitioner after we had an electro dermal screening test. They were specific to us, and everything was taken to address the imbalances in our bodies.

No drugs were used.

We took the Humet®-R initially for one month only, but still use natural vitamin and mineral supplements. If anyone wants to follow our example then please ensure you follow a personalised protocol and seek advice first.

I've had to take Humet®-R on various occasions since the initial de-tox when some of my symptoms appeared to come back, specifically after filling the car up with petrol.

On those occasions I only used it for five days and I felt fine again. Now I take Humet®-R three times a week, purely as a precautionary measure.

Another way of checking what's going on inside you is by having a Live Blood Analysis done as I mentioned earlier.

A sample of blood is taken from your finger, placed on slides and examined through a video microscope. It is looked at as though it would flow through your smallest blood vessels (capillaries) and you can see on a screen just what's happening.

A print out confirms everything and the consultant advises you what course of action you might wish to take to benefit your particular problems.

Again, this is not available on the NHS though and currently the cost for a ninety-minute test and consultation is about £150.

This also includes a saliva and urine test, and having a small amount of blood extracted from your vein for testing.

I'm certainly not claiming de-toxing for heavy metals with Humet®-R is a cure for autism. As far as I know at this point in time it isn't, but I honestly feel it's an excellent start.

I also know of another little autistic girl who's been de-toxed as a result of Jodi's experience and her mother is also overjoyed at her progress.

Lauren is six and her mother, Sally was also very ill with mercury toxicity. She too had dental work done whilst pregnant.

Anyway, Sally had her fillings removed and went on a de-toxification and nutritional programme before putting her daughter Lauren on one too.

As she was so young she took the Humet®-R every other day which is a wise precaution because of the iron content. Apparently, fatal poisoning in children under six is often the result of an accidental iron overdose.

Lauren is now out of nappies, very much calmer and has begun to talk. Admittedly she uses echolalia and her first words were ones, which Sally would probably have reprimanded a "normal" child for repeating but, as she'd never said anything coherent before in her life, it was overlooked with sheer joy.

Her teachers are impressed and delighted with Lauren too.

Some really good friends of mine also gave their autistic son Humet®-R and have noticed progress in him too.

He's much more aware of things, concentrates for longer, makes much better eye contact, and is far more vocal.

Apparently, when he first started taking it he insisted on doing everything with his eyes closed but that phase has passed.

My friend said it was really funny when she took him out in her village because she had to lead him like a blind person, and she imagined all the villagers saying, “Look at that poor woman – not only has her son got autism but he’s gone blind now as well”.

You have to laugh!

Now for the information I promised on Humet®-R. I'm telling you this, not because I have any financial interests in the product but because I was concerned initially about giving it to Jodi.

I knew he wouldn’t be able to tell me if he was feeling any side effects and I needed to be completely satisfied anything I was putting inside him was unlikely to harm him in any way.

I didn’t know whether other autists had tried it or not although I was aware many parents have tried to de-tox their children using other methods.

The problem has always been finding something that would cross the blood/brain barrier, be financially obtainable and accessible, be easy to administer and have no side effects.

Chelating can be dangerous if a person has stressed liver or renal problems because the heavy metals have to be flushed through the system as quickly as possible, and during a de-tox you should avoid sugar, wheat and dairy as these can interfere with the de-toxification process.

Well, as I told you earlier, Humet®-R comes from a peat bog which runs along the north shore of Lake Balaton in Hungary, and if, unlike me, you're scientifically minded, then I'm reliably informed it contains significant quantities of humic and fulvic acids, minor amounts of phenolic acids, calcium huminate, a degradation of lignans, shell remnants, calcareous materials, sand and other minerals in trace form.

I don't understand the significance of any of that as I dropped science as soon as I possibly could at school, but apparently some very clever people managed to make a powerful new chelating agent out of a mixture of the humic and fulvic acids.

They called it Humifulvate®.,

Apparently, humic substances have been used as mineral supplements and de-toxifying agents since ancient times, but because of modern industrial food processing, they're now almost totally excluded from the normal food chain.

However, our bodies still accidentally take in heavy metals because of the environment in which we live.

Of course we take in really minuscule amounts from here, there and everywhere, but over a period of time they build up and can affect our health.

All heavy metals are dangerous and you certainly don't want them in your body if you can help it, which is where Humifulvate® comes in.

This prevents mineral toxicity by chelating heavy metals such as cadmium, lead, mercury and aluminium, wherever they happen to be lurking in the body.

Chelating means bonding and Humet®-R is really special because it works in two ways.

Firstly, the clever people I mentioned earlier, found if they added minerals to the Humifulvate® chelate, they changed into organic minerals, much more acceptable to our bodies.

Amazingly, it's very intelligent too because it will only give you the amount of minerals your body needs, so seemingly you could never overdose.

The minerals provided by Humet®-R are potassium, magnesium, iron, zinc, manganese, copper, vanadium, cobalt, molybdenum and selenium, all of which are important to your body.

You can find out for yourself what role each mineral plays if you really want to. I don't want you to switch off by making things too technical and I don't know anyway, but I do know you need them all in the right proportions if you want to remain healthy.

You also need other minerals too, and these you should be able to get from your diet, at least you would if you don't eat the kind of self-restricted diet Jodi does.

He still only eats things that are beige or brown and dry although he will now eat green jelly. Fruit and vegetables get smelled, examined and refused, but he does have his supplements.

I know I have to get him off them eventually and who knows, maybe one day he'll just surprise me by tucking into a meat and three veg' meal followed by a bowl of fresh fruit salad. Dream on I hear you say.

Back to the complicated details though, and the second thing those clever people discovered was that when Humet®-R delivered the organic minerals, individual Humilfulvate® chelates were released.

Instead of dying away, these chelates were found to have a natural and strong attraction to heavy metals.

They just whizzed around the body grabbing any heavy metals they encountered like super magnets. Then, as the chelates got flushed out of the body in the urine and faeces they took the heavy metals with them.

It meant important organic minerals in, harmful heavy metals out - pretty clever stuff, eh?

Originally, Humet®-R was an orange-tasting syrup taken by diluting with cold water or juice. However, as it's a strong product with quite a high sugar content it can sometimes cause a tummy upset, and of course, there's always a risk someone using it might also be an undiagnosed diabetic.

Because of this, the manufacturers spent four years developing a milder capsule form of Humet®-R for daily use, which is what we all used.

When I had my full de-tox, I took the capsules for just thirty days and followed a nutritional programme to build up my minerals and vitamins, which had been badly depleted by the heavy metals.

However, some people take Humet®-R on a daily basis and use it as a prophylactic, which means they use it to prevent themselves getting ill.

I suppose that makes a lot of sense for people who are continually exposed to heavy metal vapours such as dentists, paint sprayers and those exposed to petrol fumes.

The director of the company supplying Humet®-R, which is Fulcrum Heath Limited, is called David Ward and his business partner is called Howard Thomas.

Both take it every day, as does David's ninety-year-old mother. She says it helps with her arthritis.

In Hungary, where the product is made, its most popular use is as a tonic for people undergoing chemo and radiotherapy. It appears that by rebalancing their minerals and taking out the nasties, the patients get a new lease of life.

On the information for users leaflet it says Humet®-R can be used as a general tonic to:

* Support overall health.
* As a good tonic for the elderly
* Provide optimal levels of certain nutrients
* Help maintain and support the body's immune system
* Help improve mental and physical performance
* Help maintain and support healthy iron levels
* Help the removal of toxic substances, particularly heavy metals (e.g. cadmium, mercury, lead) from the body

I can vouch for the last one certainly and if anyone wants to find out more about this remarkable product, which is NOT a drug, you can e-mail or telephone David Ward.

You'll find he's really nice and helpful, at least he was to me, but if he gets inundated with phone calls or e-mails he'll probably regret ever speaking to me.

Incidentally Humet®-R capsules are sugar-free, yeast-free, gluten-free, soya-free, GM-free and have no artificial flavours or preservatives.

They are totally hypoallergenic and are manufactured from certified BSE-free sources. How about that for a sales pitch? Maybe I should tell him I've written this story and ask for commission – (before he gets the 'phone calls).

Anyway, I guess that just about wraps things up. I hope you've found the story interesting and can now see why I think there's a real connection between Jodi's autism and my teeth.

I may be completely wrong; you'll have to decide. All I know for certain is since I got rid of the heavy metals, my health has improved tremendously and Jodi has taken some pretty amazing steps.

It may be he was just on a learning curve and would have made them anyway – I'll never know. I do know Jodi's Journey is continuing though, so watch this space.

Jodi - 3

Sorry, just when you thought it was all over I've returned. It's not that I want to have the last word, but mum took so long getting the story published it needs a bit of an update.

I'm fifteen now so you can tell mum's been kicking her heels a bit but it means I can tell you about my last year. I've improved a lot – no really, I have.

Mum even takes me out to restaurants now. Admittedly I always have chicken and chips (and the Yorkshire pudding off anyone's plate within arms reach).

I feel all the chips before I eat them although I do obey mum's request to eat them with a fork - afterwards. I can't stand different textures in my mouth at the same time you see and chips are notorious for having hard and soft bits. It's the same with sausages.

I always cut them in half and scrutinize the insides before I'll eat them. I flick out any suspect bits with a knife and discard them; then I cut off the skin and slice what's left of the sausage into little pieces, and then I make it "hot" in the microwave.

I watch the steam rise from my new acceptable sausages and eat them all up. It's a bit of a time consuming process but at least I don't rush my meal.

I like watching steam. I often make myself green jelly to eat and I love to watch the steam rise as the jelly cubes melt in the hot water.

I know by putting it in the fridge it will go "cold" and hard so I can eat it, and green jelly is my dessert most days. I have recently tried chocolate mousse though, which was "delicious" and have had lemon mousse on my lips a few times. I'm working up to actually eating it.

Being fifteen means I tower above my mum now and just last week I weighed 71kg and was 169.5 cm tall. I'm a big boy and like most teenagers my hormones are raging.

My testosterone levels are really high. The normal is between 50 and 54 and when I had my last electro dermal screening test mine was 75 so it's no surprise that I shave every day.

Sometimes I use an electric razor and I can manage that myself but it doesn't give such a smooth finish as the normal one and I always seem to have a five o'clock shadow.

Mum generally tends to shave me with a razor and foam and the last time I tried to do it myself, I cut my lip. It bled quite a bit so mum told me to put some toilet paper on it to stop the bleeding. I did – then I took it straight off.

Eventually, after I'd repeated the process several times, she told me to "leave it on" until I'd "finished breakfast". That was better. It gave me an idea of just what was expected of me and by the time I'd eaten my noodles and cereal, the bleeding had stopped. Clear instructions you see – very important to us people with autism.

We've had a change around at home and I no longer spend time in my playroom downstairs where we have a two-way mirror in the door.

You see the night before my fourteenth birthday; Daryl and mum were making a cake. I don't actually eat cakes but I do like blowing the candles out.

I used to do this with a drinking straw because I found blowing difficult. It generally ended up more of an undirected spit though and no one really wanted the cake after the candles had been blown (or soaked) out. Now I can do it just fine without any aids – must be a grown up thing!

Anyway, after I'd checked on what the rest of the family were doing I went back to the playroom to watch a video and play on my huge exercise ball.

I had a habit of sitting on it on top of the settee, which my parents didn't bother about too much because of my incredible sense of balance.

Probably about ten minutes after I'd been in the kitchen, my dad, who was home at the time, looked through the two-way mirror and saw me sitting on the settee with my feet on the ball, which was pressed up against the door.

I appeared to be staring at the mirror so Dad thought I could see him and waved. I didn't respond so he knocked on the door – still no response.

He tried to get in the room but couldn't because of my weight against the ball, and when he eventually forced his way in, he realised I wasn't responding to him.

I didn't look at him or acknowledge him and there was a graze on my forehead. On the carpet there was some blood and a wet patch.

Dad called for mum and it was immediately obvious I was confused and had great difficulty in keeping my eyes open. They concluded I'd fallen off the ball and banged my head on the floor, which explained the blood and thought I'd probably dribbled a bit.

Mum suspected concussion so Dad rang the doctors and was told to keep me awake and get me to the surgery for a check up.

As it was outside normal practice hours, we had to go to one about twenty minutes drive away as opposed to the local health centre, which is about five minutes down the road.

Mum sat in the back of the car with me, dabbing a wet flannel on my forehead and talking to me in the hope of getting a response, and by the time we arrived I was more coherent.

The doctor checked my ears, eyes and other responses and said I appeared okay but my parents should keep an eye on me to make sure I wasn't sick or anything.

We went home and my parents kept me awake for some time before I was allowed to go to bed. Dad immediately took the door off my playroom.

The next morning, I rubbed my head and said "hurt" so I had the day off school, which was a pity as I had a nice dancing role in our school production of Mary Poppins. Also, it was my birthday.

I managed my party though and blew out the candles on the cake which Daryl had finished cooking whilst I was en-route to the doctor's surgery the previous evening.

I say “party” but in reality it was just family members dropping round for a chat and some nibbles. I’ve never had a real party, and probably never will.

You need friends to have a party. I don’t have any – just the people I mix with at school and at respite care.

Anyway, things went okay for almost four months and then I had a funny turn which terrified Mum and Daryl. I went into a sort of trance, made a groan as if I was going to be sick and then my head seemed to turn round.

Daryl didn’t think it was going to stop and thought I looked like something out of a sci-fi movie. My eyes rolled, I went rigid and then shook for what were probably only about two minutes but Mum and Daryl said it seemed like hours. I then just wanted to sleep.

Daryl rang 999 because once again the local doctors surgery was closed and they didn’t know what else to do. Fortunately there was an ambulance in the area and I was taken to hospital on a stretcher with Mum holding my hand.

It was about forty-five minutes before I seemed able to speak and to register things properly and about two hours before I was back to normal.

It appears I'd suffered some sort of seizure but as it was the first my mother had experienced and I couldn’t tell her how I felt, I had to be checked out at the hospital.

My temperature and blood pressure, etc. were fine though and I was allowed to go home later that evening. Fortunately, Mum had ‘phoned my grandparents and they'd followed us to the hospital with my brother otherwise I don’t know how we would have got home.

Actually they arrived before us because the ambulance went quite slowly, which was good as it meant Mum and the paramedic in the back weren't being thrown around.

Mum had a seat belt on which made it difficult for her to reach across to me, and I was gripping her hand so tightly that had the ambulance swerved rapidly, she may have needed treatment more than I did.

When we finally arrived we had to be checked in and a place found to put me. Luckily there was a bed free so I was transferred from the stretcher on the trolley, to a bed in a cubicle in Accident and Emergency and waited for someone to check me over.

My eyes, ears, pulse and blood pressure were checked almost straight away and then we had about an hours wait to see the doctor which was quite good for an A & E department.

Mum was asked a few questions and the doctor checked to see if I was speaking as coherently as was "normal" for me.

I then had to walk up and down the corridor a few times to make sure my balance was fine but as I ran and said "time to go", I think the doctor was satisfied. Mum was told I'd probably had some sort of seizure and I'd be referred to see a specialist.

I couldn't be given any medication at the hospital then though because the diagnosis hadn't been confirmed but she was told what to do if it happened again.

They reassured her that getting me to the hospital was the right thing to do in that instance but normally in such circumstances it wouldn't be necessary.

It was well after midnight before we all got to bed and I don't think Mum slept at all that night. She wrote to dad to tell him all about it and then hit the internet to find out what she could on epilepsy. It appears it's quite common for autists to develop epilepsy during adolescence especially if they have restricted diets.

I had another seizure a few months later, which wasn't quite so frightening for Mum and Daryl as they had seen the previous one, but it took about the same amount of time for me to come to.

I was given an appointment to go and visit the epilepsy clinic at the pediatric unit of the same hospital where I'd been taken in the ambulance.

Mum took me along and explained what had happened on each occasion. She couldn't think of anything that might have triggered them off at the time though.

The specialists decided they wanted me to have an EEG which would show them if there were any irregularities in the electrical patterns in my brain – also it might indicate which side of the brain the seizures started.

They wanted to know which way my head turned which must be significant although I don't know why. It always turns to the left.

They also discussed the possibility of putting me on medication to prevent me having any more. They explained there were a few different types I could try and they would put me on a low dosage to start with and build up gradually.

If I didn't have any seizures within eighteen months then they'd see about taking me off the carbomazapine, which is the medication they thought would suit me best.

Mum wasn't too keen as they told her there could be side effects, i.e. I could become hyperactive, or I could be really drowsy and not with it. Mum had just spent the last thirteen years trying to stop me being both of those so she was naturally apprehensive.

Also, her research had indicated as anti-seizure drugs work on the brain there are inevitably other side effects, and she'd read about liver damage, stomach disorders and she personally knew of a case where patients of a particular drug were suing for sight damage. She wasn't convinced that was a route she wanted to take.

Mum explained her fears to the doctor and said she wanted to resist the drug route for the time being. She reasoned so far all the seizures had happened at home, in the evenings, whilst I was watching a video, so if the pattern continued she would always be on hand to look after me.

As I am autistic, I'm never left unsupervised and when I'm not at home, i.e. school or respite care, the people responsible for me are trained to deal with seizures.

She felt as long as everyone was aware of the possibility of what could happen, she'd rather not give me carbomazapine or any other anti-seizure medication.

She did agree to me having an EEG and asked if it would be possible to take me to see the room where it would be done and the machine used to do it. She wanted to have some idea of the procedure so she could explain it to me and possibly have a trial run or two before the big day. That way I wouldn't be so frightened.

The specialists agreed and I was taken along to see what would happen to me.

Mum asked the appropriate questions and we returned home knowing I'd have twenty-three, thin, coloured wires, approximately one metre in length, attached to my head and then I'd have to sit for about twenty minutes watching the brain patterns appear on a computer screen.

The whole process would take about an hour when you took into consideration the time it would take to attach the wires and take them off again.

Mum's heart sank but where there's a will, there's a way, and on the way home her brain was working overtime trying to think of how she could give me a practice EEG.

The answer came from my granddad who never throws anything away. His garage is like an Aladdin's Cave and he'll have just what you need – "somewhere".

Anyway, he had some old electrical cable, which had three different coloured, thin wires inside, so he stripped a long length and cut off forty-six pieces.

Why – forty-six pieces?

Well, Daryl offered to have practice EEG's too so I would copy him. That's what nice older brother's do. The problem, however, was how to attach the wires to our hair without them pulling too much as they were quite heavy.

At the hospital hair wax was used but the wires were much lighter and were attached to a machine so there wasn't the weight pulling down to worry about.

Initially, Mum tried blue tack on each individual wire, but that wasn't too successful, so eventually she stuck both sets of twenty-three wires onto a double band of masking tape, which she then placed on top of our heads.

She secured them with baseball caps and supported the wires on the back of the chairs in which we sat.

She then set the kitchen timer to go off after thirty minutes which was longer than the actual test was likely to take, but she didn't want me to get the idea I could stop after twenty minutes incase the real EEG hadn't finished by then.

The plan worked and by the time I had to go back to the hospital for the actual EEG, I was completely at ease. I knew exactly what was going to happen and the young man doing it said I was "brilliant" and he wished all his patients were as good.

The EEG didn't reveal any abnormal brain patterns though so it didn't help much in trying to discover what initiated the seizures.

Shortly afterwards I had another seizure which was witnessed for the first time by my Dad. We'd just been on a two-week holiday to Tenerife.

I'd behaved impeccably throughout and we'd had quite a relaxed time. I went swimming every day and we ate out every evening. It was sunny and warm just like a good holiday should be.

The flight and the car journey home from the airport were fine and as soon as I got in I put the tv on to watch a video. I'd survived a fortnight without seeing any and felt I deserved a quick video "fix".

Half an hour later I was in the throes of a body jerking seizure and my Mum just managed to catch me before I fell to the floor.

With Dad's assistance she lay me down with my head on one side so I could breathe and everyone watched as the electrical pulses inside me went haywire. Dad was horrified and insisted I went on medication.

He was terrified I'd be injured – not by the seizures themselves – but by crashing to the ground when one suddenly took hold of me.

He was also worried Mum might get hurt trying to catch me as I'm a big lad. He was right there though as I did give her a lovely black eye during one seizure – accidentally of course.

She had to wear thick make up for a week to conceal it, and walked around with her head down, avoiding eye contact with people as much as possible.

Despite all of this, Mum was still adamant she wouldn't put me on medication.

During the course of her research she'd discovered seizures can be attributed to a number of causes including hormonal changes, nutritional deficiencies and metabolic abnormalities, which result in the body being unable to properly utilize a particular nutrient.

She suspected I suffered from all three and as I'd been on a self-restricted diet since the onset of my autism she wondered whether it was finally affecting me.

Although I'm a big lad and appear healthy she questioned whether I was getting and utilizing all the minerals and vitamins, etc. my body needed.

She was giving me supplements but didn't know for sure they were working properly so she arranged for me to have a live blood analysis test done and in order to ensure that I'd comply with what was requested of me, she had one done too.

Our appointments were with Han Van De Braak of Integrated Medicine Practice in Market Harborough and one week prior to our testing we both had to stop taking all non-life-essential medications i.e. minerals and vitamins.

We both had to supply a sample of urine each – two actually. The first was on waking and the second was when we arrived at the clinic for the test. This was not a problem although we hadn't been able to eat or drink anything from 8.00 p.m. the previous night.

The other thing we weren't allowed to do was clean our teeth because we had to give a saliva sample. I couldn't manage that bit though as I don't know how to spit on demand and it isn't something that's easy or desirable to teach.

I've only been known to do it on one occasion and then I was told it was naughty. Mum felt it would be too confusing to teach me to spit.

The urine and the saliva were to test the acid/alkaline levels in my body and from the urine sample it was discovered I passed too much alkaline.

This apparently affects my amino acids, which in turn affects my enzymes and could be the trigger to my seizures.

You see everything you eat is either acid or alkaline forming and requires the opposite medium to be digested. In order for your body to work in its optimum way you should eat more alkaline forming food – i.e. fruit and vegetables.

Han recommended Mum check out the Hay diet, which is about correct food combination for health. She discovered everything I eat produces acid and uses what alkaline my body has for digestion, so unless I change my diet dramatically I'll continue to have problems.

Easier said than done though and it will take a lot more than Mum reading a book for me to change my self restricted diet.

I also had a heart rate test done by monitoring my heart whilst lying down on a bed and then again when I was standing up.

This took about ten minutes and the results were recorded and printed out in the form of a graph. This reveals how well your heart is working and how fit you are, (or aren't as the case may be).

Next, I had my finger pricked and squeezed. The small amount of blood that came out was pressed onto a couple of slides and analyzed under a microscope connected to a computer.

We could see the red and white blood cells moving around as if they'd appear inside the small capillaries of my body. It was really fascinating watching them wiggle about and you could see any bacteria or pathogens in between them.

The test revealed my white blood cells were active and receiving enough oxygen and my red blood cells were flowing nicely but were irregular in size.

The next test I had done was again on my blood but this time I had to lie down on a couch and have some taken from my arm. I had watched Mum have hers done so didn't mind at all when it was my turn.

This blood was also tested and we watched the results on the computer screen.

By the end of it all, I'd discovered I was borderline in the fitness stakes and could do with more exercise, had a mineralization problem and my body wasn't utilizing calcium properly.

I still had a very slight heavy metal problem, and lacked B vitamins and folic acid, which are important for most bodily functions.

I was recommended more minerals and vitamins and given some homeopathic remedies for enzyme damage and repair.

The seizures didn't stop – infact they increased in number but were far less traumatic.

Mum therefore decided to try a hair analysis test to see if that could determine how my body was doing with regard to my new minerals.

For this she had to cut off about two tablespoons of hair, which had to be clean but not freshly washed. As Mum cuts my hair herself, this wasn't a problem and she duly sent off the sample in the bag supplied by the company.

The analysis uses a method called atomic absorption photo spectrometry and enables each mineral to be isolated and measured.

The results arrived a few days later and revealed my copper levels were normal, my manganese and selenium levels were low and my boron and zinc levels were high.

Now the problem with hair tests apparently is they can be contaminated by external influences, which can give a false reading.

For instance, if you're in the same room as a smoker the hair test could indicate you had high levels of cadmium in your body, or if you use an anti-dandruff shampoo (which contains zinc) it could reveal high levels of zinc in your body, when in fact the opposite is most likely true because dandruff can be caused by low levels of zinc.

Another thing to be considered is once you cut it, hair is dead. Since I had my test, someone far more knowledgeable in these matters than herself, has assured Mum arsenic is the only reliable test that can be done on hair once it's removed from the body. I've no idea whether that's right or not, but my arsenic levels were okay.

Anyway, Mum was pleased with the way the seizures had diminished in severity but obviously not with the amount I was having and discovered they were Generalised Tonic Clonic Grand Mal seizures, which is a bit of a mouth full.

They still followed the same pattern of being always in the evening and always whilst I was watching a video on my own television.

It didn't seem to be a particular video or be related to how long I'd been watching, but the television I was using was very old and Mum and Dad wondered whether it might have a flicker they were unaware of, but which I could pick up because of my heightened senses.

They bought me a new 100Hz television, which is supposed to reduce that risk.

They also moved the furniture in the house around and I'm no longer in my playroom. Instead I am sort of centrally located so I can be seen and heard from the kitchen, lounge and conservatory at all times.

I have a very comfortable armchair to sit in and a big beanbag to lie on if I have a seizure. It's great for everyone and I'm involved in family life much more now as I'm always aware of what's going on around me.

They've also changed the light bulb in my lamp so it gives more of a natural daylight effect. This also reduces the risk of seeing any flicker on the television screen.

Still Mum wanted to find out what was going on inside me as she wasn't wholly convinced with the results of the hair test although she knew that low manganese was said to cause seizures.

She made an appointment to see Chris Mascarenhas of Highway Health Practice for another electro dermal screening test and this time I let him use my finger.

Everyone was amazed when I walked straight into the room, sat down at the computer, picked up the rod and held out my finger without any prompting.

I had to take with me all the minerals and vitamins I was taking in their original packaging so at the end of the test Chris was able to determine whether they were doing me any good, or whether I needed to increase the amount taken, or change to an alternative.

He was able to tell, just by placing the boxes or plastic containers on the machine just how the supplements were affecting me. It was incredible.

Chris recommended a few changes and now I only take six different supplements daily. Since the changes have been implemented the amount of seizures I've had has decreased and they're very mild now.

My seizures always start with me giving a loud, deep groan; my eyes roll backwards; my head turns to the left and my arms twist and go rigid by my sides. My face then contorts and I begin to shake and make a horrible choking sound.

Daryl and Mum hate that bit and make sure I'm lying on my side because I produce thick saliva in my throat and they don't want it to block my airways.

Once the shaking has stopped, Mum clears my mouth and throat and then I snore really loudly for a while before coming to.

I am always pretty drowsy to start with, generally want a drink of water and a lie down, and sometimes need to go off to the toilet so mum helps me stagger my way there, but within fifteen to twenty minutes I am usually back to normal – whatever that is.

Mind you as all of my seizures happen at night just before I would normally retire anyway, I generally go to bed and sleep them off.

Mum thinks it could have something to do with me watching videos when my brain is tired that triggers the seizures but she will probably never know for sure, just as she will most likely never know if I have any warning.

Many people report a strange smell, or a taste in their mouth just before an attack but if I get anything like that I haven't revealed it – yet!

The tests revealed watching television certainly has an effect on my brain but as watching familiar videos is my main source of pleasure, Mum is reluctant to curtail it completely.

Mum is pleased so far she hasn't had to give me medication but that wouldn't be the appropriate route to take for everyone. You have to consider all the circumstances, i.e. when the seizures occur, how often, how severe, could they be life threatening?

It appears most injuries and deaths from epilepsy are not caused by the seizures themselves but from where people have them.

Riding a bike, having a bath or being up a ladder would not be ideal situations, and of course just falling down and hitting your head on something sharp or hard could cause considerable damage.

Some people who have repeated attacks have to wear helmets to protect their heads. What a lucky boy I am!

Yes, indeed - I am lucky.

Recently Mum took Daryl and me on a day trip to London as a special treat. Her ex-boss who is a lawyer from Los Angeles came over on business and said he'd like to meet us all.

Dad was away so Mum decided I'd progressed sufficiently for her to brave the journey with me herself, which was pretty good when you consider how difficult I'd made previous excursions to our country's capital.

In case you've forgotten you can read my book called "I'm Not Naughty – I'm Autistic – Jodi's Journey".

She was confident this time I wouldn't throw myself on the floor screaming and have to be dragged, kicking, along the pavement. She was right.

We travelled down to King's Cross by train, which I loved, and then used the underground to get across to Waterloo where we met her ex-boss, Vini.

We had a trip on the London Eye, took an open- top bus tour, and went on a short river trip.

Oh, we also had a meal in a French restaurant where they had proper tablecloths and waiter service. How about that then? Okay, I admit I had fish and chips but at least it was a "proper" restaurant.

Mum and Daryl were very impressed with me and have told everyone since that I was "excellent". For someone who has autism, a condition making it difficult to cope with change, noise and crowds, that's pretty good going don't you think?

Told you I'd improved.

I still wear blue most of the time but Mum has now got me to wear jeans instead of elastic waist joggers. They did nothing for my appearance but were very comfortable and saved me having to bother about zips.

Last Christmas though, with it being the season of good will, she decided it would be good for me to wear some other form of trousers.

She bought Daryl some new jeans and decided I could try some on too. I did and we walked out of the shop with about six pairs between us – all different styles and shades of blue.

I don't know why she didn't do it years ago.

The reality is though, I wouldn't have tolerated the change then.

My improvements have been steady and progressive so take note all you despairing parents and DON'T GIVE UP!

On Tuesday evenings I go to a youth club for children with special needs. It's held in a centre for adults with disabilities so the facilities are ideal for us.

There aren't a lot of special children so it's also open to normal children who are sympathetic to our problems and are willing to join in activities without making fun or being rude and sarcastic.

It works well.

Each week we have a different activity so it doesn't become boring and it tends to rotate between a sports night where we play either football, hockey, rounders, badminton, hoops, bowls, skittles and table tennis; a pools night when we also play darts and do jigsaws.

There’s an arts and crafts night; a disco/karaoke night, a movie night where we watch a video on a huge screen and eat popcorn; and my favourite, which is the bouncy castle night when we have a twenty-four foot square castle blown up in the gym and all of us jump around at the same time and throw soft balls.

It’s great fun.

School is still going well and in September I'll be going up into the seniors. I have my transitional review soon where everyone has to decide what I’ll do when I leave Highfield.

I can’t imagine not going there, as it’s been a great part of my life since I was three and a half.

I'm very competent in many ways but I know my parents don’t think I’ll ever hold down a job.

I need lots of support and they’re hoping when I do eventually leave school, they can find some sort of opportunity for them to work from home and have me assist in some way.

I don’t know what it would be though.

It’s highly unlikely to be a bed and breakfast establishment as Mum hates cooking but perhaps we could move somewhere like Spain or France and have a holiday home attached to our house. I could help keep it clean.

Maybe we could manage a caravan park and I could keep the grounds and toilets clean. It would have to be a "No cats or dogs allowed" park though – at least it would at the moment.

You never know though, I may one day get over my fear of domestic animals too.

No harm in dreaming is there?

I haven't done much reading lately although I still do it at school. Mum has realised I don't really do it for pleasure. I read books if I have to but it's not something I choose to do and a lot of the words don't actually make any sense to me, especially things like: "but", "if", "when", "because", and all those many other words which aren't specific.

If mum asks me to choose a book to read I'll get the one with the least amount of words or one, which I could recite with my eyes closed.

I do point words out to her when we are out though and read signs – especially if I see "DANGER".

I also read the calendar everyday to see what's happening. I like to know what to expect even if it has nothing to do with me.

I still don't find the need to use a lot of language and find that I can get by really well with a few words and some miming.

My wants and needs are pretty much covered all the time so I don't really need to make the effort, but when I do want something and it's not readily available I try to make myself understood in some way, shape or form.

For instance, my brother is just learning to drive and I sat in the back seat the very first time he was allowed behind the wheel in my dad's little run-around car.

Daryl had never driven before and as lessons are so expensive we thought it would be a good idea to give him as much free practice as we could.

Needless to say he was nervous, the car had obviously been filled up with kangaroo petrol and had a mind of its own. "What's wrong with this car?" Daryl fumed, as it seemed to go in any direction other than where Dad had instructed him to steer it.

After about ten minutes I tapped Dad, who was sitting in the seat directly in front of me, on the shoulder and said "Daddy, daddy" as I waved my hands towards the steering wheel.

It was my way of telling him I wanted a change of driver and the next time Daryl got in the drivers seat, I got out of the car. I think that was pretty self-explanatory.

He has improved now though and is more confident so I am okay about getting in the back seat whilst Mum takes him for a practice drive. I'll be glad when he passes his test though so he can go on his own.

Yes, I am now a far cry from the frustrated little individual who knew what he wanted but had no way to express it – thank goodness!

My journey has taken me along the right road and maybe in a few years I'll let you know where it is leading me now.

In the meantime though, I've got to give you back to Mum. I might have known any hope of me having the last word was too good to be true!

Jean - 3

Yes I'm back again and this really, really is the last bit, and don't say you've heard that before.

I wrote this story for two reasons. The first, was because there's been a lot of general interest in Jodi's well being and progress since our initial book about him

They've been through so much and wanted people "out there" to know about it just in case they could help other mercury toxic sufferers.

This story, therefore, seemed the ideal opportunity to cover both aspects.

The problem came when I'd finished it because although it's absolutely true, it questions two very sensitive issues.

With regard to the dental profession, the story challenges the opinion dental amalgam is perfectly safe for everyone, and for the medical profession, I'm questioning the safety of vaccines containing toxic preservatives for everyone.

It all comes down to mercury in one form or another and we can be exposed to different types; Mercury vapour which if inhaled and absorbed into the blood stream can be toxic; methyl mercury which is produced in our environment and we consume via fish and sea mammals, and ethyl mercury which is used as a preservative in vaccines.

The World Health Organisation says this latter type doesn't normally accumulate in our bodies, so vaccines containing thimerosal should be safe if they're sufficiently spaced out.

Mercury vapour and methyl mercury are somewhat different however.

Various studies have shown repeated long term exposure to low concentrations of mercury vapour from dental fillings can cause all types of symptoms and can contribute or worsen neurological diseases such as Akzheimer's, multiple sclerosis and Parkinson's.

Studies also show too much methyl mercury can adversely affect the brain and nerve tissue causing vision, balance, heart and neurological problems. Whilst this does come from fish and seafood, research shows it can apparently also be produced in the mouth.

It seems a bacterium, which lives in our mouth called Streptococcus mutans, can methylate the elemental mercury used in dental amalgam.

That's a bit of a worry to put it mildly.

Mercury is highly reactive chemically and if it does become methyl mercury, many sources say it becomes 100 times more toxic to the brain and nerve tissue.

That doesn't sound too good, does it?

The World Health Organization (WHO) states there is no safe level of mercury in humans that does not kill cells and harm body processes, and if that's true then just one amalgam filling in your mouth continuously vaporising mercury, could cause worrying or even serious health problems over a long period of time.

I don't know how true it is but I read on the internet Florida's environmental regulatory agency says just one mercury filling from one tooth thrown into a lake is enough to contaminate that lake for fishing and swimming.

That makes me wonder about the bits of my amalgam fillings, which I know have broken off, and I've swallowed over the years.

At the time I remember thinking – "Oh, not to worry, it's only a bit of filling" but if those little bits are still inside me I may have to be on chelation for ever!

I must admit I'm not a committed author and don't really consider myself to be one at all. This is only the second book I've written and like the first, which came about because of peer pressure, it wasn't exactly planned.

I write my thoughts down sometimes and apparently they're readable, so when this story was initially rejected I wasn't really bothered too much. However, other people were.

I only sent the story to two publishers who both told me they loved the story very much but because it dealt with such serious issues they felt it should be balanced by professional opinion.

I can understand their point. After all, as compelling as the evidence appears to be, it is purely anecdotal.

I can't prove Jodi got his heavy metal problem from me and his vaccines any more than I can prove it was dental fillings that caused me to fear for my health and cause Bryan such terrifying and debilitating physical symptoms.

The only thing I can say for certain is once the mercury and other heavy metals had been removed from all three of us, we changed for the better. That may be anecdotal but it works for me.

Thousands of others have reported similar scenarios when they've de-toxed in some way to remove mercury from their systems, one of whom is an MP in the House of Commons.

It's still anecdotal evidence of course, but when you put them all together it does seem there may just be something in it.

The dental profession is right to say amalgam has been successfully used for over one hundred and fifty years and I'll be the first to admit my composite fillings are no-where near as strong as my original ones.

They've also given me more niggling little sensations in the short period of time I've had them than in all the years I had amalgam, BUT I don't feel ill.

When the mercury leaches out of amalgam fillings, it does so over a long period of time and until relatively recently people didn't live to be what's now considered "old".

That's possibly why amalgam's been considered so safe all these years - because people generally died of other causes before the mercury got to them.

Those people who did live for longer periods tended to be rich and were often reported as being eccentric towards the end, or having the shakes. I often wonder whether they were actually showing signs of mercury toxicity.

Until comparatively recently not many people actually had fillings because they couldn't afford them and it was usual to have teeth removed as opposed to filled.

It wasn't until the introduction of the NHS dental service in 1948 that people began to have regular check-ups and treatment.

Most people of my parents' generation have false teeth and my grandparents have told tales of people sharing teeth because not everyone had their own set.

Also once you start to get mercury toxicity build up you find it difficult to get rid of other toxins and we are surrounded with them these days.

One hundred and fifty years ago there weren't the pesticides, preservatives and pollutants that both benefit and plague our lives today.

Wherever you live in our modern society you can't escape them.

There must be something in the possibility of mercury in amalgam being dangerous to some people otherwise all dentists would continue to use it on young women, nursing mothers and children. They don't, and if there's nothing wrong, why change?

In America, which is always one step ahead of us, the Association of Trial Lawyers of America held a seminar on March 9, 2004, entitled "Mercury Silver Dental Fillings As The Next Mass Tort". That's legal jargon for saying it could be the next private law or civil wrong.

The conclusion at the end of the seminar, was that "every dentist in America" should be put on notice "that if they continue to place mercury fillings in children or young women, they may well end up in a court of law to explain why they placed toxic mercury that could, or did, harm the brain of a developing child or foetus".

That could just about sum it up for me, but another point of interest which seems to add fuel to the fire is something broadcast on BBC Radio Cambridge recently concerning a subject which was also featured in the Sunday Post on May 23, 2004 stating crematoria had been identified as being responsible for polluting the North Sea with mercury.

It appears when dead bodies are incinerated, the mercury vapour from the dental amalgam fillings disperses into the atmosphere, gets carried on the wind, and ends up in the sea where it attaches itself to algae.

This is eaten by the little fish, which are then eaten by the bigger fish and so on. The bigger, older and more predatory the fish, the higher the concentration of methyl mercury and when we eat the fish it gets into our food supply.

The situation has come to light because the crematoriums are being told they have to install expensive new mercury filters and are annoyed because they've got to pay for the installation themselves, which means their funeral costs will have to rise.

Also as many of the buildings are old listed ones, completely unsuited to change, about a quarter of them may have to close as a result.

They claim the UK government signed a convention in 1992, which commits Britain to ceasing all mercury emissions by 2020, but nothing has been done so far.

If mercury in amalgam weren't dangerous, why would that be necessary? Okay I know the heat in a crematorium is far greater than that produced drinking a hot cup of coffee but again it made me think.

Now on to the vaccine issue, and here again I can't prove anything. If all the research done by the various different so called "independent bodies" and "specialists" in the medical establishment can't agree about the safety of anything, including thimerosal in vaccines for everyone, then I certainly can't prove or disprove it.

However, since de-toxing Jodi for mercury and other toxic heavy metals, he's improved tremendously, as you've just read, so my money is on the side of it not being safe for all children.

Certainly this issue has raised it's head very prominently recently, and on March 15, 2004, articles in The Business newspaper and most of the daily papers including the Daily Mail had headlines like: "Autism link to vaccine threatens drug giants", and "Autism fear over NHS whooping cough jab".

The articles stated a new American study (they are always way ahead of UK) claims infants injected with the vaccine DTP (diptheria, tetanus and pertussis [whooping cough]), containing the mercury based preservative thimerosal, were six times more likely to develop autism than those given the version now used in the United States.

UK is believed to be one of the last developed countries to continue to use this baby vaccine containing thimerosal. It's no longer used in America, Canada, Japan, Sweden, Austria or Spain because of health fears, but France, Germany and other European countries still do so.

In America there are already lawsuits being launched by parents of "damaged" children against the manufacturers of the vaccine known as DTwP.

These run into billions of dollars and the likelihood is class actions could occur here in UK eventually. There are a sufficient number of parents who believe their children have been affected by the vaccines given to them when they were supposedly healthy babies.

I'm one of them – I just wouldn't want to specify a particular vaccine as I feel the build up of toxins in Jodi was cumulative and they probably all contributed in some way to his autism.

Some parents still feel it's just the MMR that tipped their children over the edge and JABS have many parents in their records already involved in litigation about it.

Others feel it may be a different vaccine but whatever the reason, autism is on the increase and is being described in some circles as a pandemic epidemic, meaning a large increase in cases over a large area, i.e. world wide.

Figures released from the National Autistic Society (NAS) estimate there are about 1 in 110 children with a diagnosed form of Autistic Spectrum Disorder (ASD). Imagine the figure if those who have not been diagnosed were included.

When Jodi was diagnosed in 1993 the NAS were quoting figures of 4 or 5 in every 10,000 children.

What went so terribly wrong?

Some people would have you believe it's just better diagnostic records these days, and the autistic umbrella, as it's sometimes referred to, now covers a wider range of disorders.

I don't know, but it's hard to believe if the figures haven't actually increased, how is it so many dysfunctional children previously went unnoticed.

Believe me, if you have a child with autism or one with some form of ASD you can't miss it. Doctors may not have picked it up but parents and teachers most certainly would have and even if it weren't labelled autism or ASD they would most certainly have noticed.

America's Institute of Medicine is now conducting a new investigation into claims that autism is linked not to the MMR triple vaccine, but to the use of thimerosal, which is just what my story suggests may have happened to Jodi.

Hopefully the panel of independent experts will reach a conclusion that will halt the epidemic. It could save misery and despair for so many people, not to mention a considerable amount of money in resources and care costs.

Governments are their own worst enemies if they continue to advocate vaccines are safe for all even though I appreciate their need to maintain public confidence.

I listened to a doctor speaking on the subject of the DTP on GMTV as soon as the story broke and he said the evidence against DTwP was purely anecdotal, but the NHS would be phasing out the ethyl-mercury preservative as a precautionary measure.

Since 1990, DTwP has been given increasingly early to babies and it's since then there's been a massive increase in autism.

British Health officials promised to phase out thimerosal in 1999 but clearly it is taking time. They argue the risk of not using the DTwP is that vaccines not containing thimerosal have a shorter shelf life and pose the risk of contamination from bacteria.

Infanrix, which is the mercury free version, otherwise known as DtaP is actually available on the NHS but it is more expensive than DTwP and parents have to ask for it.

The UK Department of Health claim the main reason they continue to use mercury-laced vaccines is not the cost, but that a baby receiving DtaP is twice as likely to get whooping cough as one receiving DTwP.

Whooping cough is nasty and can occasionally kill, but autism is a life-long, devastating disability, which affects not only the person with it, but all those around him or her.

It's a tough call.

One set of data that does appear to reinforce the theory of a link between autism and mercury poisoning though is from the California State Department of Developmental Services.

California has one of the best record keeping systems in the world and they released information on July 14, 2004, which said it has just experienced the first ever nine-month sustained reduction in the numbers of professionally diagnosed new cases of full-syndrome autism.

Their data doesn't include children under the age of three but those between four and six.

The significance of that bit of information is these children were born from 1999 onwards and it's from that time there was a serious effort to substantially reduce the amount of thimerosal in childhood vaccines in the USA.

Anyway, I think that ties things up. I still haven't proven anything but the story remains true.

All anecdotal evidence points to mercury being removed from our bodies greatly improving our health, regardless of how it was contracted in the first place, but having read our story you can decide for yourselves whether you agree or not.

If you consider mercury may be a cause for concern in your own life PLEASE be cautious about how you remove it.

Seek professional help from a sympathetic dentist, doctor, alternative therapist or nutritionalist and good luck.

Meanwhile, for us life goes on and Jodi's journey continues. I don't know where it will lead but keep looking - we may be back!

NOTE: AUGUST 2004 - Since completing this story the health authorities in UK have announced they'll no longer be giving babies the DTwp/Hib vaccine containing thimerosal.

It will be interesting to see whether the number of new cases of autism falls.

JANUARY 2014

It is no longer possible to purchase Humet-R, but a similar product known as Heavy Metal Detox is available from **http://www.Enerex.ca**

Note From Jean

I hope you've enjoyed this book, and if so, I'd be grateful if you'd leave a review for me, please. It only takes a few minutes and really helps other people find my work.

To make it as easy as possible just enter this link in your chosen browser and it will take you to the review page.

http://www.amazon.com/review/create-review/ref=cm_cr_dp_wrt_btm?ie=UTF8&asin=0955773636

Thanks in advance
!
Take care.

Jean Shaw

Testimonials

"I read your book Autism, Amalgam and Me and thought it was GREAT. Your true story is so interesting. I'm taking it on holiday to read again.Thankyou"
- Z Caddow, Scotland

"I really appreciated this book - (Autism, Amalgam and Me)! I have often thought that my jaw problems were due to my amalgam fillings, and now I think you've proven it to me. Thanks for all the information!"
- T.Solie Philadelphia, USA

About The Author

Jean Shaw lives in UK and started writing because of peer pressure.

She writes poetry, articles, books and has several websites and blogs.

Jean also likes interviewing inspirational people and you can listen to some of her interviews at http://www.JeanShawInterviews.com

Other Books By Jean Shaw

I'm Not Naughty, I'm Autistic - Jodi's Journey
ISBN-10: 184310105X

Autism, Amalgam And Me - Jodi's Journey Continues
ISBN-10: 0955773636

Mercury Poisoning It's Not In Our Heads Anymore - Jodi's Journey Goes On
ISBN-10: 0955773628

The GVO Story – Pure Leverage
ISBN-10: 1466363983

The 7MinuteWorkout Story
ISBN-10: 1470180464

Concerns Of Women Over 50
ISBN-10: 1477569847

Jodi Goes To The Farm (illustrated)
ISBN-10: 1482316315

Jodi Goes To The Farm (Photo)
ISBN-10: 1493741985

Jodi Goes To The Zoo (Illustrated)
ISBN-10: 1482316250

Jodi Goes To The Zoo (Photo)
ISBN-10: 1493741829

Jodi Visits The Farm (illustrated)
ISBN-10: 1493721720

Jodi Visits The Farm (Photo)
ISBN-10: 1493741527

Jodi Visits The Zoo (illustrated)
ISBN-10: 1493741268

Jodi Visits The Zoo (Photo)
ISBN-10: 1493741764

A Life In Rhyme - My Story
ISBN-10: 1495465519

A Life In Rhyme - My Family
ISBN-10: 1495492737

A Life In Rhyme - People Poems
ISBN-10: 1495492915

A Life In Rhyme - Life's Observations
ISBN-10: 1495493121

Ida Godbold - 100 Years and Counting
ISBN-10: 1499558783

Reference Sites

JEAN SHAW -autism and mercury
www.jeanshaw.com

PAM CLAYTON – mercury helpline
www.pamshelpline.co.uk

FULCRUM HEALTH LIMITED – Humet® -R suppliers
www.humet.com

HAN VAN DE BRAAK – Live Blood Analysis
www.bioterrain.co.uk

www.jabs.org.uk - Justice Awareness And Basic Support

www.autismuk.com/index1sub7.htm - MMR Debate

www.autismfile.com – Polly and Jonathan Tommey

www.vaccinetruth.org/index.htm

www.909shot.com/Diseases/autismsp.htm

www.nvic.org

www.thinktwice.com/mmr.htm

www.garynull.com/Documents/autism99b.htm

www.mmr-research.net

www.autismresearchinstitute.com

Additional Reading and References

I'm Not Naughty – I'm Autistic – Jodi's Journey
Jean Shaw
ASIN: B0039XRVZM - Kindle
ISBN-10: 184310105X - paperback

Mercury Poisoning - It's Not In Our Heads Anymore
Jean Shaw
ASIN: B005GL64BM - Kindle
ISBN-10: 0955773628 - Paperback

It's All in Your Head: The Link Between Mercury Amalgams and Illness
Dr Hal Huggins
ISBN-10: 0895295504

Health Wars
Philip Day
ISBN-10: 0953501272

What Doctors Don't Tell You: The Truth about the Dangers of Modern Medicine
Lynne McTaggart
ISBN-10: 0007176279

Immunization Theory Vs. Reality: Expose on Vaccinations
Neil Z Miller
ISBN-10: 1881217124
Lessons from The Miracle Doctors: A Step-by-Step Guide to Optimum Health and Relief from Catastrophic Illness -
Jon Barron

Eliminating Toxin Overload Safely - Ian Solley

Chronic Fatigue Syndrome or Chronic Mercury Poisoning? - Candida's Fire – Jeff Clark - http://www.cfspages.com/story.html

Gut and Psychology Syndrome: Natural Treatment for Autism, Dyspraxia, A.D.D., Dyslexia, A.D.H.D., Depression, Schizophrenia -Dr. Natasha Campbell McBride

Autism File – Polly and Jonathan Tommey- http://www.autismmediachannel.com/

Toxic Tooth Talk – Pam Clayton - www.pamshelpline.com

Mercury Poisoning – The Undiagnosed Epidemic – David Hammond

Mercury – The Silent Killer – Pam Tootal